Erik Jensen's impressive diplomatic career, which involved postings and missions around the world from New York, Geneva and London to Bahrain, Pakistan and Bangladesh, East Timor, Nigeria, Chad and Western Sahara, culminated in his appointment as an Under-Secretary-General of the United Nations. He holds degrees from Oxford and Harvard and honorary doctorates from Connecticut and Seoul and has been a Senior Associate Member of St Antony's, Oxford, Visiting Fellow at the LSE and Warburg Professor in International Relations at Simmons College/University, Boston.

He has written several books including *The Iban and their Religion; Under the Sun* (as Erik Jay); *Western Sahara: Anatomy of a Stalemate; Where Hornbills Fly* and *The Struggle for Western Sahara*. He was an original Fellow of the Borneo Research Council and is a Fellow of the Royal Geographical Society and sometime Member of the Royal Insititute of International Affairs.

In his memoir, Erik Jensen recalls his peripatetic early years, his personal mission to Sarawak and a long career with the United Nations. Always listening and learning, Jensen visited many of the world's trouble spots in pursuit of peace. His story is richly observed and reflective yet is lightly told, with flashes of humour, and always completely absorbing.

Cover photo courtesy M. Bentz

ALIEN ALOFT

*Unravelling identity in
pursuit of peace*

Erik Jensen

Foreword by Colin Thubron

ELSP

Published in 2020 by
ELSP

Origination by Ex Libris Press
www.ex-librisbooks.co.uk

Typeset in 10.5/14 point Minion Pro

Printed by CPI Antony Rowe
Chippenham, Wiltshire

ISBN 9781912020133

CONTENTS

Some reviews of Erik Jensen's book *Where Hornbills Fly* published in 2010:

'I have just read a lovely book about the Iban ... which anyone who has travelled to Borneo would love ... With apparent total recall, reminiscent of Paddy Leigh Fermor's *Time of Gifts*, he evokes the wonderful life of the 'ulu', which is sadly largely forgotten today. I recommend it to all who know Borneo already and to those who will understand so much more of what is left if they read it before they go.'

Robin Hanbury-Tenison, *Traveller*, April 2011

'A vivid narrative of the ups and downs of community development ... the sheer power of Jensen's prose draws the reader into the rain-forest world of the Ibans ... this is a must-read for those interested in the hard realities of the development experience in tropical socieites and for those with a commitment to an applied and engaged anthropology.'

Victor T. King, *Asian Affairs*, Nov. 2011

'It's as freshly written as if he were remembering yesterday, full of the incongruous, arresting details ... that bring a book to life.'

Mick Herron, *Geographical*, March 2011

'a sage and enthralling account ... deserves to be read in toto both as the testimony of a remarkable pioneer and as a testament to an easily maligned people.'

John Keay, *Literary Review*, December 2010

Foreword

by Colin Thubron

ERIK JENSEN'S MEMOIR is not only lucidly and sensitively written, but conveys a genuine sense of importance, however modest the author's claims, and of adding something of note to its (inevitably scattered) areas of involvement. Personally I had only a shadowy idea of his United Nations activities, but they are powerfully conveyed here, not only in his Polisario initiative (however disappointing) but even in Bahrain, Pakistan and East Timor. This was a little like the experience we all have of reading obituaries and thinking: 'How remarkable! I never knew that about him (or her).' His Borneo years were familiar to me from his earlier book, *Where Hornbills Fly*, but it was good to read of them again.

Erik Jensen's relations with others are intriguing and sometimes unexpected, from his assessment of Kurt Waldheim and his honouring of Vittorio Winspeare, to passing sketches such as those of Siegfried Sassoon and even Aung San Suu Kyi. And his Oxford years (let alone his Heidelberg experience) start to read as valuable historical reminiscence. The author's memory is clearly very fine. And his childhood, wartime and schoolboy pieces are beautifully done (especially in their Danish dimension).

Alien Aloft is clearly the work of a *rara avis* in public life these days (or probably any days): a man of integrity and sensitivity, looking back with gratitude and sadness on a career of wonderful dedication and rich variety.

August, 2020

1 Early days and Hitler's war

'AREN'T YOU GOING to give your Mummy a kiss?' The schoolmistress urged the little boy, who had been extracted from the weekly film-show, the only thing he enjoyed. With Laurel and Hardy he could laugh away the awful weather, the unpalatable food, the improvised dormitory in former tea-rooms. And now he had been dragged back to reality. His mother used his infant nickname and moved to embrace him. 'Don't call me Buzzie – and don't speak Danish to me' he said, drawing away. His mother began to cry; his father, a naturally affectionate man, unsure what to do or best to say, suggested: 'Will you come and see us tomorrow, at the hotel?' The mistress was quick to give approval and the boy said thank you very much and raced back to Laurel and Hardy just as the film was ending.

Next morning he and his younger brother were taken to their parents. The smaller boy hardly spoke and when he did he could barely be heard. His father gave him sixpence to buy what he would with his sweet ration; all he could say was 'We have to save for the war'. The mother never forgot. In all honesty what I really remember from north Wales is largely blank and altogether bleak. If I have used the third person it is to emphasise how little of that time has been permitted to survive in my memory.

The year in which Hitler had come to power was the year I came into the world. It was not a difficult delivery according to my mother. She was jubilant at the birth of her first born, a son, twelve decorous months since marriage. She watched snow falling softly outside the maternity clinic in the heart of Copenhagen, reassured by the attention of her favourite obstetrician, a man she favoured so much as to give me his as my middle name. She was equally reassured by the love of my father. Together they returned home afterwards with baby me to celebrate Christmas. It was a very happy time, they both said. Neither gave thought to Hitler.

After taking his degree at Copenhagen university my father had been ordained in the Church of Denmark. He was pleased shortly after marrying to be offered a curacy in one of the pleasantest parts of the capital. His own father had been a country schoolmaster who played the organ in the parish

*My father's official
photograph*

*Treasured drawing of
my mother from her
time in Paris*

church where he was an active member of the congregation. He died before my mother came to know him. She did know my father's mother and his two sisters; it was not a happy experience. She had returned not long before after spending six months in Paris where she had been sent to be finished, learn some French, and encounter a little of the world beyond Odense. She was a lively, pert young woman with fair wavy hair, a good figure and well-turned legs, and Paris bestowed a taste for fashion. She did not learn much French but the memory of France endured in the charming little portrait drawn by an artist in Montmartre, which she always kept to remind her. Mild sophistication, including newly fashionably cropped hair, apparently offended the sisters-in-law – or they just did not like this fun-loving young girl luring away their beloved brother. Whatever the real reason hurtful words were said, unforgivable and unforgettable and never to be repeated even to us. My mother and her sisters-in-law did not meet again, aunts known to my brother and myself only by name and later there may have been cousins not known even by name.

My mother's own father was still alive despite losing his devoted wife as well as his fortune. He had been a successful merchant, became rich enough to acquire a house at one of Odense's best addresses, and to retire early. But, like so many, lost his money in the great depression. He had invested heavily in a shipping company that went under. He did not long survive his losses. For the remainder of her life my mother harboured a nervous horror of any and all stock market investment.

I never had the opportunity to know my grandparents and I learnt nothing about earlier antecedents, in all likelihood solid peasant stock on both sides. But Danes like to believe

Little Danish boy in his sailor suit

themselves descended from adventurous sea-faring Vikings and as a boy I enjoyed embroidering that bloodline with romantic episodes including the occasional illegitimate aristocratic input.

Three years into his curacy, in 1936, my father accepted a posting in

London. As chaplain to the Danish Legation (in the days before all became embassies) he was to minister to the substantial Danish colony at services conducted in Marlborough House chapel since the days of Queen Alexandra, a Danish princess when she married the Prince of Wales, and especially to work with Danes involved in merchant shipping at British ports. The Danish Lutheran church was theologically close to the Anglican and my father, a liberal churchman, welcomed the prospect of furthering ties through the Church of England's Council on Foreign Relations. With two small children and a maid the family looked forward to five or six years in the great metropolis and to seeing the sights of England. They settled into the house provided in south London. After spending a happy summer holiday for their second annual leave on a sunny beach in Denmark, they returned. They believed Chamberlain when he proclaimed 'peace in our time'; like many others they refused to contemplate another great war, and that Denmark might be involved.

When, in September 1939, war was declared my father pored, incredulous, over newspaper reports. He filed cuttings; those he did not judge as deserving further study he deployed as under-carpeting – we were to discover years later when we found these fascinating time capsules. Aged five years I was old enough to want to know what war meant and what this war was about. My mother explained: a man called Hitler, who desired more land. We had a plot adjoining the garden, vacant; I suggested giving that to Hitler. Too late. Hitler's army was already marching across Europe on its way to the channel.

Bombing was to cow London prior to the invasion and bombs were expected nightly. Everyone who could leave town was urged to do so, schools were being moved and the children billeted on large houses around the country. Like refugees in other lands our father, who enjoyed the relative privilege of owning a car, piled on a cot and bedclothes, packed his wife and two sons inside, and drove west. The countryside was curiously silent, the silence of anticipation, the silence that precedes the moment when action erupts. Hotels were closed, 'for the duration' it said on noticeboards. When I asked my father the meaning of 'duration' he was unable to say.

By the time the family reached Somerset we two little boys in the back could no longer be calmed. Our father began knocking on doors to enquire whether it might be possible to rent a room for his wife and small children. He judged well the houses. At the second, or it may have been the third, approach, an unpretentious manor house in middling repair, an Englishwoman looked him over, sniffed, said how reluctant she was, but 'yes'. She had quickly concluded that these evidently well-brought-up people were much preferable to the compulsory billeting of working class children from the slums, already announced.

Whether Lady Hussey was divorced or a widow or her husband on active service was never disclosed. She and our mother did not become close; their only frank exchange of views occurred when our mother enquired what was possibly to be done with all the apples rotting in the orchard and was told brusquely that she ought to realise they were being sold for cider, which served to put her off cider for life. Some two months later boys and mother went back home; nobody cried. That was the phoney war. London had yet to be heavily bombed and many people began returning. The blitz, when the docks blazed for all Europe to see, was to follow.

By then the six-year-old that I was had started school. Over the school blazer I wore a cardboard box suspended from a cord. This was obligatory. The box contained a gas mask. Gas had been deployed as a weapon, with gruesome consequences, toward the end of the first world war and the British government sought to protect children. Whether the rudimentary mask from the improvised container would have been effective was, fortunately, never put to the test. Meanwhile arrangements were already being made for our preparatory school to be evacuated away from the city. My parents, as soon as they heard, were appalled at the thought of a just six-year old being shipped off to boarding school in unknown territory and they did not want him separated from his even younger brother. They faced an agonising decision. My father had his position, his duties in London and my mother was already preparing to undertake voluntary work. London was undoubtedly dangerous and if, as they had to envisage, something were to happen to them, they concluded that their sons might have better prospects if more fully absorbed into English society. When the headmaster agreed, as an exception, to take also the younger brother, the boys would at least have each other for company. The two little school-boys, numb with anxiety, were taken to Euston Station and loaded onto a train to north Wales together with a mass of others wearing the same school cap and blazer.

Weeks passed in something of a coma. The main school was being installed in an old hotel, the little boys of the Annexe, those in their first year, were housed in what had been the Llugwy Tea Rooms. The place was cold, damp and unwelcoming. In Bettws-y-Coed a summer tourist trade had been the mainstay of the economy until war broke out. The people were Welsh-speaking, fanatically nationalist with fierce dislike for the English, whom they admitted only as money-dispensing tourists to their beauty spot as it was described in travel brochures. Rationing ensured that the food was barely edible; the boys learnt to eat whatever they were given. High tea did not deserve the adjective; only bread, a scrape of margarine and a touch of jam survived. Jam was rationed and to prevent those who were greedier from consuming more than their share, each boy had his jar for the month, labelled with his name. Given the privilege of choosing, instead of boring raspberry or strawberry, I opted for greengage only to find that after two weeks of greengage I wished it were just either strawberry or raspberry.

The monotony, if not the misery, was relieved towards the end of the first term. A boy had been belatedly admitted when his father, a naval officer, was posted. On his second day the new boy developed chicken-pox. It spread like wild fire. The entire Annexe, where no one had already had chicken-pox, fell ill. Dormitories were improvised as sick bays, the teachers pretended to be nurses and the boys struggled not to scratch where it itched so terribly. As a souvenir only a few indistinct scars survived. Parents were reassured, when it became necessary to advise them, that the outbreak was under control and the boys were beginning to recover.

The weather did not improve. Clouds hung low over the valley, thick and gloomy, dripping wetness on everything between the enclosing soaked, green-grey hills. After prolonged rainfall the tea-rooms flooded to the boys' entertainment as well as discomfort. An air-raid brought some excitement, or what was claimed to be an air-raid when a stick of bombs fell in a field close to the hotel that housed the main school. Spitfires pursuing an off-course German Dornier had driven it so low as to be skimming the roof-tops and the pilot, suddenly faced with a mountain, released his bombs to gain the lift necessary for clearing the range ahead. He cleared the mountain before being shot down. The weekly film-show provided the only other excitement.

Shortly after the chicken-pox epidemic subsided, and the air-raid, the boys' father had been able to save enough of his meagre petrol ration to drive to north Wales. He and the boys' mother were thrilled at the prospect of seeing their children again. It had been a difficult time for them both, that they had been unable to help when the boys were ill, that they were never there when needed, and the obligatory Sunday letters ('Dear Mummy and Daddy, I hope you are well') revealed nothing. But the reunion outside the improvised cinema proved far from the joyful moment they were so much looking forward to. They returned, miserable, to the hotel and the mother cried most of the night. Whether or not the boys should be addressed by childish, foreign-sounding nicknames or spoken to in English, whatever the terms, their mother was not about to abandon them. She would stay in or near Bettws-y-Coed. The father, poor man, would have to return alone to London and the air-raids. Lodging was organised but the arrangement was doomed not to last and after a couple of months both mother and boys journeyed home on the irregular war-time train service, every carriage blacked-out, through un-named stations. Colourful posters had been replaced by warnings about enemy agents and notices that 'Careless talk costs lives'.

War continued but despite the bombing life in London gradually resumed. After the worst of the Blitzkrieg was over the preparatory school reopened a branch in its old buildings and those parents who wished were able to move their sons back from north Wales. Raids, if not nightly, were all too frequent. Watching the searchlights had the merit of providing entertainment, as long, thin bands of light moved awkwardly across the sky, bumped into each other, crossed over or came together in a choreographic overture to the fireworks that followed. Anti-aircraft artillery rarely brought down a plane but it inhibited low altitude precision bombing. Targets had long since moved beyond the docks, military and industrial sites to the landmark buildings of Baedeker air-raids and indiscriminate destruction of London and other cities with a view to breaking civil morale. For us children perhaps the most disagreeable part was being removed at night to the shelter that had been built by my father, with some informal assistance, to withstand a collapsing house though not a direct hit. The shelter was miserably cold and damp and my brother and I, sleepy and comfortably warm, only wished to be allowed to die in our beds. It must have been worse for our parents who sat cramped into the space alongside our bunks. Sirens, the wavy wail of warning especially, seeped into the subconscious, never to depart. The unwavy all-clear was much like any siren call. Incendiary bombs burnt the wall-flowers fronting the French doors, but spared the fuchsia perhaps out of respect for its historic German association. Less amusing were the blasts that more than once shattered windows or blew out replacement cardboard. But I do not remember being afraid. We collected shrapnel for fun, unconscious of the appalling damage to human tissue the jagged metal posed.

English prep school boy being formed

My brother and I slept through a time bomb falling near the entrance to the house one evening when both our parents were out. They were appalled on returning home to find their way blocked. Our no-through road had been cordoned off. A policeman barred access because, he explained, of unexploded ordnance, a time bomb. No one was allowed to pass, he added politely but firmly. My mother, almost hysterical, insisted she had to be allowed through, her two children were alone in the house down the road. That's where the bomb is, the Bobby said, which only made her more distraught. My father was told to leave his car but they were eventually permitted to walk home to where the two boys were still innocently sleeping. The time bomb, just across the road, was defused the following day. To our boyish disappointment we were kept well away, not allowed to watch even from a distance.

We had no relatives or close family friends in the armed forces but we knew civilians who were killed and more than one family whose house and home was destroyed, and we saw with our own eyes the widespread destruction caused by bombing. And I remember when my father came back one day, white-faced, to say that after an air-raid he had made his way through broken glass and rubble to find his car with a shoe on the running-board: the shoe had a foot in it. Almost worse than bombing, from a child's angle, were the boils we suffered from (Job's problem was well understood), the chilblains endured in winter and ghastly food, unimproved every morning by the obligatory teaspoonful of neat cod liver oil (capsules an unwarranted luxury), not to mention sweet and chocolate deprivation.

In 1943 'Doodlebugs' provided our own close encounter with real war. Dr Goebbels' named his retribution weapon, 'v' for 'Vergeltung' in 'revenge' for 'V' for victory and they were officially 'v1's, but calling them 'doodlebugs' displayed English unwillingness to be cowed and it described them perfectly. If they demonstrated Hitler's advancing technology they did not show it: an outboard-engine mounted on a bomb with baby-wings. They flew low, visible and highly audible. Their distinctive brr-brr was not continuous, but intermittent, with short pauses. No resumption of brr-brr and the doodlebug hovered an instant before falling, straight down. They did as much damage if shot in the air so, except for those that could be destroyed over the channel, were allowed to fall wherever the engine cut out. Air-raid sirens announced their passage. So frequent these became that people ignored them. Schoolchildren had to comply and we spent so much of the day trooping in and out of shelters that the headmaster decided to end the term in early summer. The weather that year was lovely. My brother and I were deployed in the garden to watch over a new-born sister and monitor approaching doodlebugs. Only when the flight path loomed overhead was action expected. It happened one afternoon. Our mother, alerted, grabbed the baby from her pram, shuffled my brother into the shelter and, just as the engine cut out she and I became blocked both trying to squeeze through the doorway when the bomb exploded. Quite near: on the parish church.

After the doodlebug incident my father decided, since school was closed, that it would be healthier for his sons in the country. He knew a Danish-born landowner with a farm in Norfolk, who was prepared to have my brother and me billeted. We loved the open countryside and roamed at will with no one to object. The few farm labourers were those too old for military service, and they talked with a pronounced regional accent, at times quite unintelligible. The only one closer in age to ourselves was an adolescent farm boy, as ill at ease with well-spoken Londoners as we were with him. He demonstrated how best to dispose of unwanted kittens by smashing the adorable babies against a brick wall. Then sneered when we looked ill at ease. He did not mind killing, he said; he wanted to kill Japs. He did not tell us but his father was a soldier with the Norfolks, the regiment that had disembarked in Singapore straight into Japanese imprisonment and the ghastly tortures of the Burma railroad.

The nearest village was within walking distance. New Buckenham was quiet, not a single car and nobody in the deserted square. From the smithy wafted the pungent smell of charred horn, and I stopped to stare, fascinated, as the blacksmith nailed a steaming shoe onto the hoof of a great, docile carthorse. Did I want anything? he demanded when I went on watching, so I wandered away from the hiss and smell. A cottage at the edge of the village had a well-maintained garden, with many butterflies flitting between flowers. They were beautiful. Ineptly I tried to capture one in cupped hands when it flew over the hedge. In the attempt I stumbled against the garden gate. The gate flew open and from the garden a voice boomed: 'What are you doing?' An elderly man appeared. I apologised politely and profusely. He asked where I was staying; we spoke the same English. What was my interest in butterflies he wanted to know, did I collect? I thought them beautiful and hoped to learn about them. He began to explain before inviting me to return the following afternoon when he would show me more.

Next day I was asked into the cottage where a doctor's surgery had been adapted, after he retired, as a study with specially designed cabinets the length of one wall. In every cabinet drawer after drawer was filled with butterfly specimens, perfectly set, mounted and ordered by family. I was overwhelmed. The man told me where the butterflies came from and how rare some were.

His enthusiasm was infectious and I left infected by the old doctor's passion. Butterfly-collecting was a serious hobby in those days and encouraged. It drew me to the study of genetics, of classification, the spread of species and more. And I learnt the delicate process of setting and mounting specimens. It now seems appalling to have killed these lovely and harmless insects. But it endowed me with a heightened appreciation of the natural world and some ability to identify, or recognise the family, of extraordinary butterflies that I have had the great joy of observing over the years in Asia and Africa as well as Europe – and drawing them to the attention of locals who often considered butterflies of little account.

Before we left the farm our parents came for a weekend. They arranged to stay in a tiny village house whose owner was absent on war-work; she was the young wife of a junior officer in the Norfolk regiment. I discovered his ceremonial sword and was fiercely reprimanded for removing the blade from its scabbard and wielding it to determine how serious a weapon it was. It would be another year before the war ended and some months after peace in Europe before the defeat of Japan. And long after that before the few Burma railroad survivors of the ill-fated Norfolks could be repatriated.

The family returned to London. We were greeted by Hitler's crowning technological achievement, a rocket capable of being blasted from the continent across the channel and into London. It was more technologically brilliant than it was effective in defeating British resolve. No air raid warning was possible making it less disruptive of ordinary life and without generating tension like the doodlebugs. When it exploded you were dead or you weren't. But the rockets did considerable damage and people were also killed in the blast. They would have provided serious and increasing intimidation had the destruction of launch sites in northern Holland not been achieved. Fortunately, Hitler's technology had limited range and the launch sites could not be repositioned further away as the allied armies advanced across the continent.

Meanwhile my brother and I were thrilled by graphic adventure stories from occupied Europe. Our father was active in supporting the free Danish movement in London, spoke patriotically on BBC overseas service broadcasts to Denmark and received in our house Danes who had been smuggled out from behind German lines. One described the torture to which as a heroic saboteur he had been subjected before being rescued in a dramatic raid involving extraordinary precision bombing by the RAF and coordinated soldiering: his 'favourite' the electrified 'dance-floor'. Another was a politician who recounted his escape in a fishing-boat concealed under a load of cod. This was the man being groomed as foreign minister in the Danish government for the moment German control collapsed. He was to be parachuted in and was given parachute training. When that broke his leg I inherited the bicycle, which even in London he deemed a necessity. Unfortunately, not only did it lack the latest Sturmey-Archer 3-speed gear to which I aspired, but it had a back-pedal brake, a device that I considered far from sophisticated, and difficult to operate. His adult son, meanwhile, impatient to join the war effort, had been commissioned in the Grenadier Guards. Just before fighting ended he was killed by a sniper when standing beside his armoured vehicle after a successful engagement, while his father was returning to take office in Denmark.

My mother's war work focused on supporting the large number of Danish seamen and others serving under allied flags or who had enlisted in the armed forces. They told of U-boats and attacks from the air and the wild north Atlantic, they all deserved great admiration, she insisted. She was less enamoured of the heroic Anders Lassen, for good reason excessively pleased with himself, who proudly displayed the gap where teeth had been knocked out in close combat; he had already won MCs and would go on to a posthumous VC. Denmark was the only non-Commonwealth country to win VCs in both world wars; in the first it had been Karen Blixen's brother.

2 War ends, school continues

On 5 May 1945 German forces surrendered in Denmark and days later Germany capitulated, leaving the victorious allies to contemplate what remained. The war had ended. My parents, elated that it was over, were pleased to feel they had contributed to the allied war effort however modestly and both valued the decorations bestowed upon them by the king of Denmark.

A child's life followed its established pattern. Education soldiered on. Usually we bicycled to school up the Old Church Street in once fashionable Upper Norwood and, before free-wheeling down through Sydenham, passed where the magnificent Crystal Palace stood for decades having being resited from Hyde Park after housing the Great Exhibition of 1851. A catastrophic fire in 1936, following which it was not rebuilt, marked the culmination, many said, of the Victorian world; Churchill, on his way to Chartwell, is reported to have stopped, awed by the blaze, and with tears in his eyes state that this confirmed the end of an era. Crystal Palace declined to being a bus terminus and home-ground for an eponymous football team.

Victoriana survived on Church Street where an imposing hotel stood. I wondered who the guests of the Queen's Hotel could possibly be since I never saw anyone arriving or leaving. Yet it had been, during the decades when the Crystal Palace housed great exhibitions, distinguished concerts and manifold important events, a well-patronised residential hotel. Very many years later I was in another part of London waiting for a friend to finish dressing. To pass the time I picked up a book about Richard Burton. Folded inside the cover was a hand-written letter of several pages and it was signed, by Richard Burton. The letterhead had The Queen's Hotel in Upper Norwood. I was very tempted to remove the letter and in retrospect I wish I had. It was a rented house and in all likelihood the book would have disappeared and the letter almost certainly lost like much else of Burton's own writing.

With the boys returned from North Wales Dulwich preparatory school came fully back to life. Soon after war's end the whole country, and with it the school, was animated by a General Election, the election that would determine what kind of country post-war England should become. My parents were not political. When I asked about the parties, Conservatives and Labour, and what they stood for, my father somewhat naively explained Labour as being in favour of giving everyone an equal opportunity. That concept of fairness was enough to convince me to lead the pro-Labour mock campaign at school, which smacked of class disloyalty and I was vastly out-numbered. But, of course, Labour did win and set about changing English society – maybe for the better.

The days were numbered when a master teaching English language would illustrate differences in usage with reference to train passengers waiting at the station: those about to enter the 1st class carriage said 'What an obnoxious odour', those at the 2nd 'What an unpleasant smell' and those at the 3rd 'Wot a bloody stink'. We were still taught and expected to speak the King's or BBC English, with a gentleman's Oxford accent. Perhaps because my parents spoke Danish at home I was acutely sensitive to the particularities of English usage as I heard it not only at school and absorbed the language as my own. Quite obviously not everyone spoke the same English, accents varied and vocabulary; Nancy Mitford's 'u' and 'non.-u' was self-evident well before she published. It mattered, that was equally apparent. Nor did that disappear despite the changes that post-war Labour government inflicted on British society. At home my brother and I always spoke English; we understood the Danish that our parents continued to speak but, for us quite naturally, we replied in English. All we missed from an English upbringing were Beatrix Potter and the Train books and perhaps some of the nursery lore and folk superstition that nannies and grandmothers were reputed to impart.

Rationing continued unabated. Neither nationally nor personally was any major change immediately apparent. My parents remained under no pressure to move from London but the prospect of my father returning to a living in Denmark did begin to loom. And with it my further schooling. Pleased though our parents were with the school at Dulwich, and they were delighted, that would not continue as an option if they left England. My father decided to send me to Denmark. Although there is not quite the same tradition of boys' boarding schools as in Britain two or three prestigious establishments existed. They were patronised by the families who believed in that form of education but principally by Danes serving abroad as diplomats or with one of Denmark's great international companies as well as the sons, it was becoming the case, of divorced couples.

Herlufsholm had a particularly fine reputation and it was to the headmaster that my father wrote, failing to recognise that Denmark had just emerged from years of occupation, isolated, and was far from the outward looking country it had been and would again become. My father's wartime activity was not as well-known as he liked to believe, and he may have been unnecessarily honest. To the headmaster he wrote that his eleven-year-old son had excellent command of English, had several years of French and Latin and had made a good start with Greek apart from doing respectably in mathematics and other subjects; his Danish, however, was limited. The headmaster replied that Latin and Greek at that age were not part of the curriculum, even French; knowledge of English could be useful but Danish was essential for a boy to be considered for admission to the school. To my father's fury there was no attempt to seek an accommodation, to propose entry after immersion in a Danish-speaking environment for a while, or to suggest tutoring.

My father made an appointment with the English preparatory school headmaster. John Leakey was a remarkable man. He had been a mountaineer who still enjoyed country sports; he had conducted a highly successful evacuation of his schoolboys at the outbreak of war under the most challenging of conditions, made a success of wartime schooling and brought everyone back together in Dulwich. He was proud of his school's achievements, the merit scholarships won to leading public schools and increasing demand for entry. He listened courteously when my father explained the difficulties encountered in planning my further schooling in Denmark. It did not make Leakey unhappy. On the contrary, he wanted me to stay. He thought highly of me, he said, and it was his hope, no conviction, that I would win a scholarship to one of England's great schools. And he did not wish fees to be an insurmountable obstacle.

The die was cast, English schooling would continue with opportunities for me to exploit, not that I particularly enjoyed school. If children are presented to me I avoid strenuously anything that smacks of my own experience when faced with an adult's 'Where do you go to school?' 'Do you like it?' The polite response was 'Yes, thank you, Sir,' which was commonly followed by the adult's 'Wish I was back at school. Happiest days of my life.' I remember the gloom that engendered: the suggestion that life would become progressively worse; schooldays were not that bad but they were bad enough. In later life I have encountered very few people who really enjoyed school that much. But if I cannot claim that my schooldays were the happiest of my life there were many good moments, especially in the world of books. At home I was an avid reader, the typical boy stretched on his stomach and impossible to wrench from the world of his imagination. *Treasure Island, Coral Island,*

The Young Fur Traders, The Gorilla Hunters, Lorna Doone and Robin Hood stories, anything about Red Indians, Vikings, pirates and cavaliers and that involved swords, bows and arrows absorbed me; I had no taste for guns and little interest in aircraft.

I was in the school library steering clear of G.A. Henty, whose many works occupied two shelves with tales of high adventure under the imperial flag. I preferred seeing myself as a Viking. But I was actually looking for a book entitled *Eric, or little by little.* Boys used only surnames, that was how we were listed, addressed and known, but Christian names did not necessarily remain secret. The great majority, John, Michael, Bill, Tom, Harry, Dick and all, attracted no attention. Those with a less usual name did. Julian and Eric were two names to appeal to the privileged classes in mid-Victorian times but Eric, except in Scotland, lost status and went out of favour. Good-looking with fair, wavy hair I was teased: with 'little by little', for no obvious reason, made part of the ribbing.

The book, I had discovered, actually had Eric as hero, the handsome, clever, athletic, popular boy who goes down-hill after he smokes! It had been published in 1858 as a didactic tale, written by a later Dean of Canterbury, and proved immensely successful. By the middle of the twentieth century it was almost forgotten; there was not even a copy in the boys' library. But the subtitle, misinterpreted, survived. And Eric as a name was demoted to the flat cap wearing class; the working class cartoon character Andy Capp has an Eric for friend. That Eric was not to be confused with my Erik with a 'k', an entirely different affair, which meant Erik the Red and other Nordic heroes also called Erik; Stockholm's patron saint was St Erik.

I was leaving the library, having failed to find 'Eric, or little by little', when the door opened. In marched the headmaster, this was an era when encounters with the headmaster were usually triggered by a misdemeanour and threatened the prospect of being caned. When he asked what I was looking for I wondered what I might have done wrong, avoiding Henty could appear unpatriotic. I thought it safest to say: 'I was just looking for something to read, Sir'. Come with me, he said, and I followed into his private study where boys rarely went except to be admonished. I passed from the rough readiness of school premises, chalk dust and a medley of vaguely unpleasant smells, into an elegant, well furnished room. An impressive desk occupied prime position between antique chairs; against two walls imposing glass-fronted bookcases glinted behind comfortable seating. French windows overlooked a well-tended lawn; no schoolboys were anywhere to be seen. I was left awed and wondering while the headmaster moved to one of the bookcases and took out a fine leather bound volume. Here, he said, handing me Kipling's *Puck of Pook's Hill*. Read this, and when you have finished, tell me what you think, and I'll give you another book. Other books by Rudyard Kipling followed and not only Kipling.

Leakey listened to my comments, discussed them with me, encouraged me to think for myself. He took increasing interest in my school career as a whole and authorised the staging of a play I had written ambitiously in blank verse, with the story line derived from elements of Lorna Doone, the Zorro films and my imagined heroic pirates, which served, incidentally, as a swash-buckling vehicle for my acting ambitions. The text does not survive – fortunately. Some school prizes do. Among others I won the reading prize and was called upon to read the lesson at prayers and to speak to visitors. This model 'English' boy advanced to become head of his house, the Chippeway (the houses were named after Indian tribes and the head known as tribe leader) and ultimately head boy, captain of the school.

For secondary education, when my parents expressed a preference for a London school, Leakey said the two most esteemed, both ancient foundations, were Westminster and St Paul's. He proposed that I sit the competitive scholarship examination a year early for the experience and I went to Westminster. The school, next to the Abbey, was approached through Dean's Yard and I revelled in the historic surroundings. The following year, 1947, for the moment of truth, I was inscribed for the examinations at both Westminster and St Paul's. St Paul's happened to come first and I found myself in West Kensington, where the school had been moved after a fire many years earlier at its premises beside St Paul's Cathedral, housed in a notable example of Victorian architecture and surrounded by playing fields.

I was awarded a foundation scholarship on the endowment of John Colet who had been Dean of St Paul's in the early sixteenth century. As one of that miraculous draught of fishes, Colet's scholars, I would have received a silver fish for my watch chain before watch-chains ceased to be part of a schoolboy's uniform. Leakey withdrew my name from the Westminster exam; St Paul's was considered academically the better school, and predominantly for day boys, which my parents preferred. I was equipped with a white shirt, semi-stiff detachable collars and collar studs front and back, and cuff-links as well as grey flannel trousers, now long trousers, and the black school blazer. Even without the watch-chain I was no longer a child.

School-days began with prayers in the great hall. Prayers were said in Latin, some were attributed to Dean Colet himself and one or more to the 'learned Erasmus' of Rotterdam, the great European humanist of the Renaissance and Colet's close friend. We were believed to be the only school in England where many of the original Latin prayers were still in regular use that had been said daily and without intermission since before the Reformation. The English Church Christian ethos, which had been the founder's inspiration, and provided the motto '*Fides et litteris*', continued to pervade the school. Roman Catholics, of whom there were a few, and Jews did not attend prayers but were otherwise assimilated in the life of the school. St Paul's differed from the other great British public schools by not being principally a boarding school; in everything else it conformed. Games, as sports were sensibly known, were important and among the boys more prestigious than academic achievement. The importance of games was bolstered by the conviction that team games, in particular, encouraged certain qualities. The most valued were football – rugby football – cricket and rowing. In all these the team not the individual predominated: in rowing most of all since an oarsman who rowed 'better' than others in the boat was as much a disadvantage as the one who rowed worse. Sport was believed to foster team spirit but also to develop the leadership qualities appropriate to an officer class.

Alongside academic work music and art as well as other activities were encouraged, including acting. Occasionally plays were performed and, after winning a school reading prize, I was offered a leading part in *The Rivals*, as Mrs Malaprop. But what I remember best was the annual Colet Clubs Revue. St Paul's sponsored and supported a boys' club in the impoverished East End of London and the Revue was to raise funds. It was a light-hearted affair with sketches written by masters as well as boys. One year I was on the same billing as Jonathan Miller; he already looked somewhat like Danny Kaye and he emerged as the star of the show with a hilarious imitation of Kaye and Tubby the Tuba. Long decades later, when we happened to meet at a Shakespeare commemorative event in Stratford-on-Avon, Jonathan said he remembered, claiming to recall that performance, an early precursor to his brilliant career in the theatre, more as a producer than an actor.

The Revue was performed in the school's great lecture theatre. This was where we were also assembled to listen respectfully to eminent speakers. One of the most famous was an old boy. Field Marshal Viscount Montgomery, as he had become, was not only a St Paul's old boy but had used the buildings as his headquarters late in the war. It was here that plans were developed for the invasion of occupied Europe. Monty told us how pleased he was to be back, though he did not look it. He began by referring to the unimpressive record of rugby's First 15 that season; his own team had been very much more successful. You win matches before going on the pitch, he said. As in battle. You won before going into action. He recounted at length his exploits in the north African campaign, was totally dismissive of the Italian forces but respectful of Rommel and the Germans, a worthy opponent, fair contest and worth beating, making it sound like a rugby match. Montgomery was a hero and we were meant to admire him, but boasting was not considered good form. I was much more impressed shortly after by Field Marshall Earl Wavell, who quoted light-hearted Latin and snippets of favourite poetry, verses he remembered by heart and he thought worth reciting. When Viceroy of India he is famously reported to have asked 'Has anybody seen my Browning?' meaning the poet not the gun.

School societies flourished. The Milton Society, John Milton had been at St Paul's, was prestigious and met occasionally for readings in the High Master's presence. I was invited to join and flattered to be chosen President. Among the most active was the Pi-squash (the name a survival from an era where squash was schoolboy slang for a society; pi, I assume, a disrespectful reference to pious). I had been hearing of great house parties, at Easter and in the summer holidays, but I took some persuading before agreeing to inscribe myself.

Presiding at Milton Society annual feast, Walker Library, St Paul's School

The Pi-squash house parties had their origin with an old boy of the school, employed as an underwriter at Lloyds, who had been greatly influenced by the moral rearmament movement in the late thirties. He was unmarried, conservative and upper middle-class; it is hardly necessary to mention that he wore tweed and smoked a pipe. He was a convinced Christian of the non-demonstrative school, on the opposite pole to Billy Graham, and this was the Christianity he sought to propagate. He began with Sunday afternoon meetings where Christian themes might be lightly discussed but the emphasis was on Jesus the friend, as convivial togetherness. From that evolved the idea of a house party during the holidays, entirely voluntary with time spent principally on sporting activities though without overweening competition. He identified a school in pleasant countryside to rent for a week or two during the vacation period and staffed it with old boys who had recently left school, most still at Oxford or Cambridge, and one or two like-minded slightly older individuals. No one was addressed as Sir, all were to be known by their Christian names, which was quite revolutionary for the time. Dress was entirely optional. Every evening a brief time was set aside to consider an aspect of Christianity, but that was the only indoctrination. It proved a highly successful formula and attendance grew year upon year as word spread. Whatever motivated the young men who agreed to help may be discussed but there was never the slightest suggestion of inappropriate behaviour, and real friendships developed.

John Thorn, an old Pauline who had served in the Royal Navy towards the very end of the war, was then at Cambridge. At one of the house parties I told him of my aspiration to get to Cambridge (I am not sure why, at that stage, I did not prefer Oxford) and he offered to show me round. He was at Corpus Christi College and I was especially taken with Corpus, though I also admired King's, of course, and Trinity, and I forget what more I saw of that enchanting place. Cambridge, or Oxford, was the university I had to attend.

As a scholar of St Paul's there was every expectation that I would win a place at one of the two ancient universities. At fourteen I had passed the School Certificate examination with matriculation exemption, two years earlier than the national average age, and at sixteen I was successful in the Higher certificate, the last public examination before entering the university. But scholars at St Paul's were expected to remain at school another couple of years during which their command of Latin and Greek would be further honed, enabling them to win the most prestigious prizes, competitive open scholarships to sought after colleges and acceptance for the most demanding degree courses. In addition, and in the English context this counted, they would develop and learn to exercise leadership in different aspects of school life.

My father, whose perspective was more continental, did not see the merit in paying fees to remain at school when no further examinations were needed for university entrance. He wrote to the High Master. The High Master replied at once to say how highly he thought of me and of my prospects, including the prospect of Oxford; he hoped very much that my father would reconsider – and I believe offered some financial incentive. But my father, a clergyman, had limited means, a second son as well as a daughter to educate and may have had other priorities. He decided that I should leave school; I entered the University of Copenhagen in 1950 still sixteen years of age.

3   Rootless in Copenhagen

SCHOOL HOLIDAYS HAD ENDED at Harwich. Disembarking passengers were guided to Immigration. A large sign split British Passports from Aliens. Being designated Alien affronted him, he who spoke impeccable English and behaved like an Englishman. To be more English than the English was, of course, as bad as not being English enough. People, once they discovered that you were not British born, offered condescending advice. When he asked 'do you have tickets for this evening's performance?' he was told an Englishman would simply say 'have you got?'

But if he was not English, what was he? He felt more foreign in Denmark.

I entered the university of Copenhagen in 1950 still sixteen years of age – I was to discover that the next youngest undergraduate was eighteen months older. My admission was under a special ruling that accepted foreigners holding a concluding secondary school certificate from Germany, Britain and, I think, France. They were, however, required to sit a supplementary examination in Danish, language, history and literature. But legally I was not a foreigner. I had become fluent enough in Danish to persuade the tutor for admissions interviewing me before matriculation that as a Dane I was under no obligation to sit the special exam. Although that might be true, he said, he thought I would be well advised to study Danish language, history and literature. I said yes and departed relieved and happy in the knowledge that I would not be obliged to sit an examination; I had always disliked examinations. Worse still, I was hopeless at Danish spelling.

The first university examination was a year away, far enough not to be disconcerting, and before it approached I discovered that we were to be examined orally. In England all examinations were written, with a trifling exception for the unimportant French oral. I had no other experience of oral examination and might have found it alarming had I not realised the significant advantage I enjoyed in speaking Danish, and by then I was more than fluent, rather than trying to write in a language that I could not spell.

I acquired the spoken language quickly enough, though colloquialisms, swear words, slang, even counting never came naturally. When to use the familiar 'Du' and when the polite 'De', corresponding largely to French 'tu' and 'vous', posed few problems (only when I encountered Danes in later years was I surprised to be addressed as 'du' almost everywhere – till one explained: nowadays we call everyone 'du' like the English 'you'; I failed to point out that 'you' was English for 'De' and that 'Du' translates as 'thou'). I knew next to nothing of Danish literature, with the part exception of Nis Pedersen whose poetry I translated.

The great names in Danish culture escaped me, except, of course, Hans Andersen, known invariably as H.C. Andersen. I had barely heard of Holberg, Denmark's Moliere, much less the unpronounceable tragedian, Oehlenschlager. Grundtvig might be great, but why? Kronborg, the reality at Halsingor, was a very different castle from Shakespeare's Elsinore, and Rosencrantz and Guildenstern did not sound at all like Danish names. In that I was mistaken: both were part-anglicised versions of aristocratic surnames and an Erik Rosenkrantz was actually King Frederik of Denmark's ambassador to Cromwell's Protectorate, a self-confident youthful-looking man who followed the latest fashion for shaving. When asked by Cromwell why he did not yet sport a beard, Count Rosenkrantz responded sharply that had his sovereign known it was a beard the Lord Protector required, he could have sent a goat.

Everyone who matriculated at the University of Copenhagen, whatever he or she planned to read, for whatever degree, was required to sit the Philosophikum. An ancient survival, it comprised three subjects: philosophy, psychology and logic. I inscribed myself and attended the obligatory lectures. This gave me time to reflect on what I really wanted to study; vague ideas about medicine lost substance when I attended an introductory presentation and found my English classical education useless in understanding the Danish vocabulary of physics and chemistry, which only reinforced an unstated prejudice in favour of the humanities. Philosophikum led me into philosophy. That I found stimulating and I enjoyed the reading. The rest of the curriculum was less appealing, but it provided an excellent path into more sophisticated command of the Danish language than that I acquired from daily social discourse. And I discovered my real interest in the philosophy of religion and comparative religious belief. The faculty of theology offered a course that included those subjects and I enrolled myself.

I did not enjoy Denmark. Which was absurd. Many times since I have wished the experience had been otherwise: there was so much to enjoy. I walked and bicycled in and around the capital, which is a beautiful city beautifully maintained, but I did not feel that I belonged. No friends shared my (English schoolboy) sense of humour – language was essential to wit – or adolescent prejudices. I knew no one close to me in age or background. Living at home was not helpful. That I was sixteen-years-old when I entered the university, more than a year younger than the youngest fellow student, that I had only been to boys' schools, that I had no local friends would have been easier to overcome in student accommodation. After boarding school I expected, now an undergraduate, greater independence. My father, whose student days had been austere, thought it unnecessary that his son not benefit from comfortable living in his suburban rectory.

I read avidly, mainly in English, including contemporary verse, most of which I appreciated though I was baffled by Edith Sitwell's near gibberish, but embarrassed to confess, even to myself, that I found it unintelligible. I also wrote quantities of poetry, and sent a poem to T.S. Eliot who graciously replied that he had enjoyed reading it and nothing suggested that the author was anything but English. A pantomime performed by members of the British colony allowed me temporary access to a world where I felt at home. Every summer I made my way to England, to see friends and the places with which I was familiar.

Old friends from St Paul's invited me to stay. One was exceptional in that I did not know him that well, but he was especially insistent that I spend a weekend at his mother's place in Kent. Julian Clifton-Knox had been in the same house at school, junior to me. I remembered him only because he had been an eccentric loner who did not relate easily to other boys and I had stepped in to defend him from aggressive teasing on more than one occasion.

His mother lived near Ashford in Kent. Mersham Manor was a charming old house and as I immediately discovered filled with beautiful things. I knew little about art or antique furniture but had an instinctive feeling for quality. Among the paintings I recognised the name of Alfred Stevens on a set of sketches probably related to his work as a sculptor. Mrs Clifton seemed mildly surprised that I knew of Stevens, pointed to other pictures and to the Jacob Epstein outside the window and talked to me about the artists. She seemed to enjoy discussing art, was pleased to find someone interested and sufficiently informed to appreciate what she told me. Julian was perhaps a disappointment in that regard. It emerged that Julian was an adoptive son and that his brother, also adopted, was not really his brother and a committed outdoorsman. (All of which from my more conventional background I found fascinating.) Mrs Clifton described the pre-Raphaelites as if she had known them, which might well have been true when I calculated that she, who was manifestly older than most other mothers, had been married to someone greatly her senior, a wealthy connoisseur and Victorian art patron.

On the second day of my stay I was discreetly invited upstairs where Mrs Clifton opened a bedroom door. She had something special to show me. On the walls were four amazing paintings: instantly recognisable as William Blake. I was stunned, could not stop looking at these extraordinary images, which I thought I knew from reproduction. Mrs Clifton allowed me space to study each picture minutely and the time for their splendour to seep in. I was at a loss to articulate what I felt but I did make clear how grateful I had been for this revelation in the letter of thanks I wrote shortly after departing. Those Blakes I would never dismiss from my mind but I did not expect to encounter Julian again.

Back in Copenhagen I taught English at the Berlitz school to earn money. At the director's insistence, I masqueraded under an English surname because all Berlitz teachers of English, announced as native speakers of the language they taught, had English names. Discovering that James Joyce had worked as a Berlitz teacher boosted morale. The Berlitz method came to me easily. Students liked my teaching style it appeared from class enrolments but I developed no wish to make this my career when the director offered me longer term employment.

A fellow teacher was an Englishwoman whose husband was spending a year in Denmark as an American Fulbright scholar. In the university cafeteria I chanced upon the two of them drinking coffee with other young Americans and was introduced, by my real, not Berlitz, name. When one of them tried his Danish on me I replied in an English that surprised him. Where had I learnt English, did I have an English mother? We chatted, became friendly. They told me which part of the States they were from, they were all in Denmark on Fulbright scholarships. They talked also of other scholarships, to American universities, and that gave me an idea. I had no special wish to go to America but it offered an alternative to Copenhagen. When I asked the Fulbrights about scholarships for study in the US, they referred me to the consulate.

There I was given a sheaf of forms to study and complete including names and addresses for persons being asked to provide references, which I did. At the submission deadline I was summoned to a US consular building, directed to an unimposing office where a junior official told me to sit down. She had received my references, she said and asked me for the completed forms. She looked them through, nodded, she had only one comment. Under the heading of preferences I had written Harvard. She advised me to take that out. It was best not to express a preference and let the people in New York, who would be handling applications, decide which college was most likely to offer me a place. She almost smiled as she added that she had seen the references and thought there was a very good chance of my being awarded a scholarship. I asked what objection there could be to stating a preference. She would explain, she said. If a preference was expressed my application would be forwarded to that particular college and by the time it reverted to the central office there might not be anything else available. So you see, she said, looking firmly through glasses wedged on a large nose, you should not put anything. Perhaps I did not know, she added, that there were many fine colleges in the US. But nothing in that flat-chested, bespectacled, unalluring appearance made a young man eager to follow her lead.

When she began to insist that putting Harvard only showed that I did not know enough about higher education in the States I wanted to say that the only American universities I knew as comparable to Oxford and Cambridge were Harvard, Yale and Princeton. Much as I liked the idea of a scholarship to the US, I had no wish to attend just any university. That, of course, was not what I said.

I asked for time to reflect. She became annoyed, emphasised the deadline, told me to be sensible and, when I insisted, accused me of being an arrogant young man. She had her own target, I imagine, for ensuring the submission of convincing applications. 'Think again', she tried in a changed tone of voice in a last effort to win me over. When I did not respond she became angry, shuffled my papers together, thrust them at me, saying come back – if you want to be sensible.

I took the file home, the references as well as my own application. The references were confidential and I was not supposed to see them. When I read what my old headmasters had written I barely knew how to react. They said such flattering things about me, the kind of person I was, what I had already achieved and my potential; I was tempted to read them again and again. In the English school tradition undiluted praise was virtually unheard of.

My prospects for a scholarship to the US seemed hardly in doubt and I saw no reason to present my application without a preference. The American Fulbrights included one who had been at Harvard and while telling me about life in Cambridge, Massachusetts, he mentioned the Episcopal Theological School on Brattle street, where a friend of his was studying. Whatever the formal relationship to Harvard there was official course-sharing, that he knew, and it would be a congenial place for a student of theology, which I was, and who was an Anglican. It sounded right though I may have read more into the Harvard association than was warranted. I completed my form accordingly and presented it to the consular official for onward transmittal. She took it, ungraciously.

That summer I was back in London where I called on my old High Master. Dr James received me warmly, pleased to hear that his recommendation had been successful when I told him that a US scholarship had been approved. Take a degree while you are there, he said. Was that possible? I asked. He thought it might be. If I could obtain a degree he would assure me of a place at Oxford and he believed I would qualify for a St Paul's closed exhibition to help with fees. I was jubilant. That was my dominant objective: to go up to Oxford. You had only to look at the back of the Penguin books published in that era to see where the authors had been to school and university. Almost all those I admired were Oxford educated with a few from Cambridge. Eliot set the bar even higher with Harvard and the Sorbonne as well as Oxford.

Travelling to the United States in the early fifties was for the privileged, if impecunious, few. The dollar reigned supreme and out of reach for Europeans still war-impoverished. Cheap flights had yet to be invented. Visa requirements and other formalities were not made easy. You were required to present an X-ray to prove lack of tuberculosis and a Wasserman test showing that you had not been diagnosed with syphilis. Sea passages, travel by air remained the exclusive preserve of very important persons or the very rich, were provided for those awarded American grants or scholarships. And special visas, which had to be collected in person.

The vice-consul's office had the Stars and Stripes on a mini-flagpole beside a large picture of the president. I was asked to wait while he processed a woman who was engaged to be married to an American serviceman and was travelling to join her husband-to-be. The nature of their relationship appeared something of a mystery as she spoke no English. She did not understand a word when asked to swear that she would not attempt to assassinate the President and I was asked to interpret. With coaching she achieved an 'I do' sufficient to satisfy the vice-consul before it was my turn to swear. This was many years prior to Kennedy being assassinated. But one did wonder whether someone bent on murdering the president would be intimidated by the oath. Next, I was asked my race. That was the first time I encountered such a question. 'European, I suppose', I said. The vice-consul wrote 'Caucasian', a category to which I had not previously known I belonged.

The ship on which I sailed to America in 1953 carried no self-confessed would-be presidential assassins, we had all been subjected to a Wasserman test – so no syphilitics – and we all had with us an x-ray to prove we were not suffering from TB. But few had much money and, even with those guarantees, the opportunities, the openings in that less confident pre-pill era were restricted, relations between the sexes more traditionally scripted. The great majority of passengers were students, either Americans returning from study abroad or Europeans with scholarships to the US. An impoverished post-war Europe and on the other shore a bloated American dollar ruled tourism out. Most of those on board rose early to admire the Statue of Liberty as we sailed into New York before disembarking to encounter the new continent as hundreds of thousand immigrants had done over time. We faced none of the huddled masses diversion to provisional holding centres or risked being shunted to Welfare Island for disease control. Visas were rapidly processed and stamped. On the quayside Customs looked through the declaration before opening my trunk containing the normal student equipment, clothing and books, plus a small packet that I had been asked to deliver to Boston by a Danish relative of the addressee. Inside the beautifully be-ribonned box was a token gift, a brooch, I had been told. That the customsman wanted to see for himself.

He tore off the ribbon and wrapping paper, opened the lid, and when he took out the brooch we both saw under it another shiny item, a second small brooch, which was not listed on the declaration. I said that I had not been told of this. The customsman, unimpressed by that explanation, felt he had unveiled a small-time smuggler. Everything, so meticulously folded and packed, was thrown onto the rough surface used for the inspection, every last item was removed from the trunk. I took comfort in not being fined as I laboriously replaced my belongings as best I could. I had arranged to share a cab to the station with another young man. He, an American returning home, insisted on routing us through Times Square. Though I said nothing, Times Square seemed no match for Piccadilly Circus, now aglow following the war, with Eros freed from boxing. But I was impressed by Grand Central Station, the star-spangled ceiling of its palatial booking hall.

4 American outlooks

In Boston I was met by a student from the Episcopal Theological School, where I was to live. My trunk fitted easily in the boot of his car, which he called the trunk – and I learnt that the bonnet was not a bonnet but a hood. Few students in Europe had cars of their own and none on that American scale, whatever the bits were called.

ETS enjoyed fine premises on Brattle street at the edge of the Harvard College campus. The day after arriving, with no one to watch, I rendered homage in the Yard before John Harvard's statue, the ritual act required in conformity with student superstition to promise a degree. The university's administrative offices were easy to locate and I wasted no time in enquiring about a one-year postgraduate degree course; my three years in Copenhagen had been accepted as equivalent to a first degree.

When I asked about an MA the young woman behind the desk countered very pointedly: 'Here at Harvard it's an AM, Latin, you know'. She was not impressed when I assured her that I knew some Latin. Anyway there was no one-year course available at the Graduate School, she added sharply. She reverted to other business, picked a document up from her desk and waited for me to go. Dejected. The academic year was on the verge of beginning, time obviously short and the administrative officer had hinted at no other options. That evening one of my fellow students at ETS commiserated. He thought it might be worth approaching directly the Harvard Divinity School, despite its Unitarian associations.

Next day I established that the Divinity School offered three Harvard degrees in theological studies, all at the postgraduate level: a three-year bachelor, a one-year Master's and a full doctoral programme. But would I be considered as qualified for admission to the Master's? It was an advantage that few foreigners approached American universities in those days; circumstances could be handled without reference to precedent, on their individual merits. I had three years enrolment in Copenhagen's theological faculty, with examinations passed in Greek and even Hebrew as well as philosophy and comparative religion. In admitting me they may have chosen to overlook that

I was only nineteen-years-old. Speaking English as I did could have helped, as English education commanded respect. People in the Boston-Cambridge area, it seemed, were either anglophile, the clear majority, or distinctly anglophobe, usually those of Irish extraction. Only when I wished to attend the reputed St Patrick's Day parade in Boston did my fellow students demur. So keen they usually were for me to experience the sights I only understood when one said 'OK, provided you don't open your mouth or we'll be massacred'. To them I was English and Ireland's most hated.

Work for the degree followed the American pattern of courses, four each semester, followed by a comprehensive examination at year's end. I felt privileged in being admitted to a seminar at the Harvard graduate school conducted by Professor A.D. Nock. Nock was a Cambridge educated Englishman who had made his academic career at Harvard; his book *Conversion* was a brilliant study that opened my eyes to the distinct religion that Christianity was. Judaism was essentially tribal, an inherited identity. The religion of both Greeks and Romans was rooted in time and commonly place; the inhabitants of a given city venerated their gods or deities and visitors would be expected to worship them also. With Christianity came the novel notion of personal faith, that one's religion did not derive from tribal identity or where one happened to be living. Individual conversion to the exclusive Christian belief opened the door to access for any person anywhere while simultaneously blocking easy accommodation with all other religious observance.

Exploring the Mediterranean world at the time of Christ allowed me to understand much better what evolved into Christianity and what it made sense, for me, to believe. This was developed further through a course with the distinguished Professor Henry J. Cadbury after first taking koine Greek with him. He had me write a paper on Albert Schweitzer's *Quest of the Historical Jesus*. Whereas I idled over koine Greek I focused intensely on Schweitzer (such an extraordinary man, a fine theological scholar, a gifted organist before qualifying in medicine to launch his hospital in disease-ridden west Africa) and relished the time devoted to absorbing his argument and distilling it into an essay. That Cadbury approved of what I had written gave much satisfaction; he too was a man to respect, a noted academic but also the representative who received the Nobel Prize on behalf of the American Quakers for all they contributed during the war.

Nobody explained the American system to me and the importance of course grades; to the Americans it was self-evident, what they had always known, and few foreigners entered their orbit. Not knowing otherwise I assumed that what counted for the degree was the final year-end examination, as would be the case in Britain and on the continent. I treated course work as I had treated lectures and the occasional seminar, with commitment when I was stimulated and casually when not inspired, which was hardly geared to ensuring straight 'A's. For the comprehensives I disciplined myself thoroughly poring over examination papers from past years that revealed the range of questions and the depth of knowledge expected. I sat the papers in my own rooms following Harvard's 'honor system'. Well prepared I wrote confidently in answer to every question posed. In 1954 the master's degree was conferred. It was already months since I had heard what really mattered from Dr James. He confirmed that I had a place at Oxford, at Worcester College, which he believed would be an excellent college for me. St Paul's would award me a Viscount Campden exhibition, the name somewhat grander than the monetary value justified, but appreciated nonetheless.

The academic experience was but a part, a lesser part in many respects, of the American experience as a whole. As a nineteen year-old I was significantly younger than my fellow students at ETS and I enjoyed novelty status as a foreigner. I met with much kindness and generosity and some allowance for eccentricity. The early fifties were a difficult time in America characterised by the McCarthy witch-hunt. I was proud of the new president of Harvard, Nathan Pusey, for having the courage to stand up to bullying tactics and I almost cried during the Army hearings when the brave lawyer challenged McCarthy to his face. To a not very-politically-sophisticated me McCarthy was so patently objectionable that I had difficulty in understanding why anyone supported him.

But many Americans did. Within days of my arrival a fellow student had asked me where I expected to spend Thanksgiving. I barely knew at that time what Thanksgiving represented and had no plans. Would I come to his home? I thanked him and largely forgot the invitation in the maelstrom of new friendships and relationships of the weeks that followed. He was not among those I came to know well and I was slightly surprised when, shortly before the Thanksgiving holiday, he reminded me of the invitation. I had been asked meanwhile to a more congenial place but thought it right to honour the earlier commitment.

His parents, it emerged, were working-class Americans and proud of their only child who had made it through college and been accepted for a higher degree. The father was a long-distance truck driver and acted the part. He ensconced himself in a well-padded easy chair in the sitting-room, confronting a large television set, with his beer in one hand, and, only when reminded by his wife, did he offer a can of beer to the guest. Conversation, such as it was, meandered from questions about family, differences between his country and mine and the weather before touching lightly on current affairs. An English-speaking visitor may have made him defensive, and when I said that I did not understand the support McCarthy apparently enjoyed, he was off. McCarthy was great, he was America's champion in the war with communists, how could you fail to see that? Everything he did was designed to rid America of these Commie infiltrators who were sneaking in all over. Neither son nor wife argued with him and I dropped the subject. It was not the most convivial Thanksgiving, but it had been interesting to experience a working-class home, to be offered coffee with the turkey at dinner and milk as a drink.

Sunday lunch in the affluent suburbs was otherwise. I was invited to join a friend's parents after church. Following a glass of sherry we were seated in the dining-room round a traditional table, laid with fine silver, served quality beef and offered wine – as well as water, of course. The conversation, such as I remember, revolved round the choice of preparatory school for the younger son. 'Preparatory schools' in the American system were fee-paying secondary boarding schools and equivalent to English Public schools, though not as generally patronised. 'Where were you at school?' the standard introductory question in England at that time referred to secondary schooling: not in America where, I quickly learnt, it applied to college.

After lunch I was asked whether I might enjoy a look round the surrounding countryside. With pleasure, I said, and was told that the daughter of the house, a high school senior with plans for Wellesley, would be delighted to drive me. We passed well-manicured suburban gardens and a country club before approaching a park where my driver stopped in the parking area beside an ornamental lake. When I made to open the door she wanted to know where I was going. A walk? She expected to stay put, to park. In my vocabulary that was not a journey's end in itself. But there were people visible in most of the other parked cars overlooking the lake, young people it appeared and actively involved with each other. We parked and I much enjoyed my exposure to local countryside customs.

America, certainly the Boston Harvard world, was a surprisingly conformist society. They laughed when, shortly after arrival, I asked whether there was any uniform requirement at the university, for so it appeared. Of course that is what I would ask, they said, because I came from a country with conventional dress codes, but this was America. Though incidentally, I was discreetly told when they noticed my footwear, only Negroes (then the acceptable term) wore suede shoes. With that exception, despite their insistence on diversity, on freedom of choice, the vast majority of students were clothed according to an identical dress book: tweed jackets, of the distinctive American weave, cut with a single truncated vent, and flannel trousers in winter or seersucker and khaki drill in summer; shirts were broadcloth button-down and ties striped in the English club tradition. Although crew-cut hair was not general all hair was kept short. That provided my first confrontation. Barbers were relatively expensive, I had limited means and husbanded my resources. Since I had no objection to slightly longer hair I postponed having a hair-cut until the day I found on the dormitory noticeboard an invitation to contribute to 'Erik's Haircut' with a small money-box beneath.

Before leaving Cambridge I thanked the faculty members who had shown me kindness. First, the distinguished scholar of comparative religion who had insisted on my coming for coffee after his lectures; his wife presided, a beautiful woman from South Carolina, who looked the southern belle and talked with the most perfect accent from *Gone with the Wind*. When I said thank you, after drinking a cup of coffee for the last time, I could not resist adding how much I had enjoyed simply listening to her speak. She broke into a peal of laughter; one reason, she said, she had loved my visits was just listening to the way I spoke, it reminded her of Leslie Howard, the film-star then at the height of his fame.

Before the academic year reached its final close my friend, John Heidbrink, reminded me of the near-forgotten commitment to spend time as a counsellor in Northern Michigan at a summer camp. I had little idea what this entailed but agreed because it would at least provide my keep and enable me to see another part of America. Greyhound bus routes, which spanned the United States, were inexpensive and you could travel at night instead of paying for a hotel. I slept between rest stops when passengers relieved themselves enthusiastically before consuming milkshakes or hamburgers. I even acquired a taste for milkshakes.

The camp in Northern Michigan was sited beside a lake in open woodland. An experience that I had looked forward to without enthusiasm turned into one of the most enjoyable of my year. This was the episcopal diocese's summer camp and it attracted well-brought up young people. They welcomed me warmly. The high school girls especially, lively confident American adolescents, made a great fuss of this twenty-year old Harvard graduate who spoke like a film star. For ages after my departure I continued to receive their flirtatious letters, with envelopes mysteriously inscribed CU with L and K.

I sadly said goodbye to the summer campers in Northern Michigan and a final farewell to the many other friends I had made. Of course, we would be writing to each other, even visiting. There were invitations to stay: from San Francisco to New York. In New York Rumsey Ellis' wife said she was sure that her father would be delighted to put me up before my departure. Days later came the response: 'Daddy would be only too pleased though unfortunately he would have to leave on business soon after my arrival. But I was more than welcome to stay and would be looked after.' Daddy, it emerged, lived elegantly on Park Avenue and introduced me on arrival to his manservant; I had only to ask for whatever I needed.

As guest of Tom Chesterman's family in San Francisco I was less spoiled but generously received. Everywhere I went people showed extraordinary hospitality. I could not imagine this in any other country and I found Americans immensely likeable. But I had no desire to become an American. The year had given me a sense of identity. I was English-speaking; that suggested a link with America. But I recognised myself as old world European, as belonging to an ancient culture evolved from classical Greece and Rome through the Renaissance and the Enlightenment to the present, and perpetuated in monuments, traditions and manners, even aspects of the landscape. The United States had many things to recommend it but lacked the inspiring, encompassing rootedness of 'old stones' as one American friend described Europe's architectural heritage. Oxford had old stones in glorious abundance.

5 Oxford, as it was

WORCESTER COLLEGE'S HEAD PORTER, big and burly, with traditional bowler hat and moustache, conformed perfectly to type. He called you 'Sir' while making it entirely clear who was in charge. I was referred across the street where I had been assigned a room in a college building. My scout was Mr Parvin; he would help me with my luggage. Billy Parvin showed me the room and brought up my trunk. 'Where are your boxes, Sir?' he asked not once but twice. He associated me, I later discovered, with Georg Jensen of Bond Street and expected at least a tea service. Billy became more immediately friendly with the man allotted the room next to mine; they shared betting tips on the horses.

I met my neighbour late that first afternoon when he came to my door, said his name was Mike Scott. He was immaculately dressed in a double-breasted grey flannel suit, his Brigade of Guards tie jutting from a white cut-away stiff collar; he reeked of Trumpers cologne. Was I planning to attend the meeting that evening to which all new members of the college had been convoked? he asked. Yes, I said, of course. Would I mind awfully telling him what transpired over a drink next day; he had a party in London. And with that he set off.

Two days later I found a pair of suede shoes in my room. Billy Parvin, said he knew very well that the shoes were not mine, they belonged to Mr Scott, who had asked that they be deposited with me. What was all this about? I enquired when I saw Mike on the stairs. He hoped I did not mind, just for the day. His father was coming – and his father disapproved of suede shoes, although they were much in fashion at the time and worn by nearly all who could afford them. After that first inspection I never heard of further parental control or found any shoes temporarily parked.

Mike and I shared a bathroom with the third occupant on our landing but had little else in common. His father was an intelligent man who had risen to the heights of British industry, marrying a Guggenheim en route, but Mike had not inherited his father's intellect or what one might have imagined was his mother's family affinity for the arts; he did have another gift, as an outstanding cricketer. He had kept wicket for one of England's top schools and would do the same for Oxford. Mike made an early gesture of friendship by inviting me to meet his sister who would be dropping by with a friend. The real purpose, of course, was to link Mike and the friend. It failed. The friend and I took immediately to each other, leaving Mike with his sister to talk to.

Unlike Harvard, official Oxford imposed a dress code. For Hall, dinner in the evening, jacket and tie were required and a gown. A gown was also necessary for tutorials and university lectures. For examinations and more formal occasions we had also to wear 'sub-fusc', a dark suit with a white shirt, white bow-tie and tabs. At most other times we had complete freedom of dress and the variety would have appalled Harvard. Roll-collared pullovers worn year round and in every context vied with the aesthete's exquisite neckwear and extravagantly tailoired trousers and suits in emulation of Edwardian gentlemen, though emphatically not to be confused with fashionably working-class Teddy Boys.

Oxford in 1954 half-tried taking up where pre-war Oxford left off. We were too young to have fought in the war but old enough to have experienced air-raids and war-time privation, to endure rationing and to revel in its eventual ending. We aspired to resume English university life as it had been and as we thought it was supposed to be. We emulated *Brideshead Revisited* without the glossy highlights and with the volume at a lower setting; few undergraduates were wealthy with the government making a point of pruning the wealthier families. But we dressed and behaved in many respects not unlike the pre-war generation.

Worcester College benefitted from having as provost one of Oxford's great personalities. J.C. Masterman, later to become Sir John, had been an undergraduate at Worcester before the First World War, played cricket, hockey, tennis and fives at an international level, and been a don at Christ Church until his election in 1946 as head of his own college. To be at Worcester, with its gracious way of living as J.C. himself described it, was a great privilege, not least while he was provost and as such unrepeatable. His style, imposing his personality, has since fallen from fashion. He led the college as he thought right, was personally and decisively involved in the selection of new members, with a policy designed to produce balanced men and a happy college. It was. The undergraduate body met a high academic standard but was not over-scholarly, the college fielded successful teams in most sports but was not dismissed as hearty and members showed a healthy interest in other activities, social, dramatic, musical and literary.

Michaelmas term passed all too quickly, learning Oxford's ins and outs and discovering some less obvious beauties, taking a beginner's part in college activity and making friends. I had little wish to leave when term ended though the prospect of Christmas with my parents, brother and sister was attractive enough. Danish Christmas had great charm and Copenhagen was among the first, if not the first, city to create the perfect formula of pedestrianized areas in the centre of town with Christmas decorated streets and shops. All in impeccable taste, even the music. I was busy organizing travel as cheaply as possible when Billie Parvin announced a visitor.

A young man, wearing the uniform of the Royal Canadian Air Force, arrived. He smiled. It was minutes before I realized this was Julian Clifton-Knox. Since visiting Mersham I had not had any contact with Julian. He invited me to lunch at the Mitre, Oxford's most prestigious at the time and beyond my means. He had an expense account, he said, and I would be his guest. Both the Canadian uniform and the expense account were unconvincingly explained over lunch as related to a filming project in which he had an investment. In that same connection he was due to spend a few days in Paris shortly and would much appreciate my joining him.

Term was ending but I was sorry to say that was impossible. Julian insisted that I could be of great help and my costs would be covered; an aeroplane ticket would await collection. I was not sure how much of this to believe but my ticket from London to Paris was at the airport and I met Julian at the designated hotel. He introduced me to a man and woman said to be working on the same project. I was then left to my own devices, which in Paris is far from disagreeable. Next day we talked about arrangements and I was invited to dine that evening with Julian and his business partners. Following last minute adjustments we met for a brief drink but not dinner; something had cropped up, which Julian promised to explain in the morning.

The following day I asked to be put through to his room. He had checked out said the receptionist. For the rest of the day I waited patiently, but nothing, no message, no call. The twenty-four hours following initiated me into being deceived, to being more than embarrassed, to being without travel funds or money for food and to becoming increasingly hungry. I counted my pennies, quite literally. The change I had just covered the hotel room and, with some assorted coppers, including Danish coins earmarked for Christmas, I persuaded a travel agency to issue the cheapest available train and ferry ticket; the agent generously took a few pence off the price to make this just possible. Near starving – ogling menus outside restaurants only made it worse as food and drink became increasingly an obsession. After nearly two days without food I walked to the station and eventually staggered back to London and my savings account. I saw no value in tracking down Julian. Some considerable time later I encountered by sheer chance on a London street the man and woman to whom I had been introduced in Paris. They remembered our meeting only vaguely. What news, I asked, of Julian? Nothing. They hardly knew him, it emerged, the briefest acquaintanceship only. Then the man took the evening paper from under his arm and pointed. 'Ah, but had I perhaps seen this?' A longish article reported that a Clifton-Knox had been found guilty of fraudulent bank transactions and sentenced to imprisonment. He had succeeded in convincing his bank manager, who knew of his assured inheritance, to advance substantial credits and authorise transfers, using as security highly valuable paintings, believed to be original Blakes. What caustic verse or threatening image William Blake might have made of this. Oxford seemed reassuringly traditional when, after Christmas, I returned.

Of the college societies best known was The Buskins. The Buskins acted. They had been putting on amateur dramatic performances for many years and had a well-earned reputation for their successful summer productions in the College gardens. I was invited to audition – it had become known that I acted at school – and to my great pleasure was invited to become *jeune premier* in that summer's production of *The Tempest*. Some tutors disapproved of acting because of the time taken with rehearsals. Mine was unconcerned; I think he believed that organising time was my responsibility, though whether he was right I am less sure. I did too little work but had a wonderful time playing Ferdinand opposite an enchanting Miranda.

The performances, in Eights Week when Oxford attracts family, friends and old members in abundance, were a great success. This should not be entirely attributed to the perfect weather. The college 'Gentlemen's Eight', in which I rowed, was conspicuously successful: we bumped every day and won our oars. And in the evenings I acted. The production is remembered partly because our producer emulated a trick to have Ariel dance away over the lake. Boards had been positioned just below the surface and, happily, Ariel never slipped. Ariel went on to become a bishop prior to retiring as a monk, which may or may not be relevant. Calaban was to become Rector of St Mary's, the university church, before going over to Rome. Naturally, the non-spirit players had more conventional careers.

Papist and monk acted citizen and wife in the following year's *Knight of the Burning Pestle* where I played the youthful lead Jasper opposite a suitably attractive Luce. Jasper's stage pursuit of Luce spilled over into real life. Luce had already accepted an invitation to the Magdalen Commemoration ball

Oxford, Worcester College, Buskins production in the gardens by the lake of The Tempest *and* The Knight of the Burning Pestle

and, unable to disentangle herself, challenged me somehow to arrive. Not easy. Gate-crashing was expected at Commems and the most elaborate security arrangements were put in place, so elaborate that it became a sport to evade them. I reconnoitred access points to Magdalen. The most obvious, along the river, would be heavily policed but I wondered whether the high wall to the rear of the deer park might be left without elaborate guarding. On the day of the ball I dressed in white tie and tails, only my shoes were not correct evening dress but I needed rubber soles to climb the wall and descend discreetly on the other side. The deer scattered when I bumped down and I waited for them to settle before advancing tree by tree to a low fence at the park's edge. I jumped and landed calmly on the path when there seemed to be no one about. But from the shadows a man immediately emerged, raised his bowler hat and asked very politely for my name and whether it was on the guest list. I said it wasn't and he directed me to a small side-door leading out into Holywell.

At two in the morning fully evening dressed I was not ready to retire. I walked round to explore the riverside approach and in passing observed a ball guest emerge through the porter's lodge, go to his car parked nearby and return straight past the porter. It was quite some minutes before anyone else came out. I took the chance: gave just long enough for an unspecified errand and strolled confidently into Magdalen through the porter's lodge; the porter barely looked up and never noticed the shoes I carried low on the far side. Once within the college I changed shoes in a dark staircase and went to the ball.

Luce was nowhere to be found in or around the various dance floors. During my search I noticed spot checks being made and was at pains always to be appear coupled when inspection threatened. And finally I discovered Luce in conversation with the man who had invited her. She was more than surprised to see me, sought to disguise any emotion and introduced me casually to her partner. I smiled a knowing smile then disappeared into the crowd and, having recovered my shoes, out of the college with a great sense of accomplishment. Jasper deserved a bow.

The Lovelace Club was more ancient than the Buskins. It had been founded in 1884 to perpetuate the memory of Colonel Richard Lovelace and to further the study of letters. Lovelace, who had been a member of the College, when it was known as Gloucester Hall, had his magnificent full-length portrait hanging in the Provost's lodgings. Very good-looking, superbly dressed and as romantic a figure as one could ask for. He had fought for the royalists during the civil war, been imprisoned for supporting the king, and written unforgettable poetry, including the lines 'Stone walls do not a prison make, Nor iron bars a cage'. The Lovelace Club in my day concentrated its study of letters on a twice-yearly dinner at which a distinguished literary figure was invited to speak. I cannot be sure how it happened but I found myself elected president. The president was expected to invite the speaker, for which the provost's blessing was necessary and I approached J.C. before writing to T.S. Eliot. Musty club records had Eliot reading *The Waste Land* at Worcester in the late twenties, but that was long ago, and the provost had no hesitation in agreeing: he would ask Eliot to spend the night, and did I have his private address? I was pleased at the prospect of meeting the great poet, which would also provide me an opportunity to thank him in person, and in English, for his generous response to the seventeen-year-old who had sent him some verse.

Two weeks before the dinner a letter arrived from Eliot, very apologetic, to say that he was unwell and regretted being unable to come to Oxford. I went straight to the provost. J.C. knew, he had already heard from Eliot, who was really sick. What was I to do, at short notice? J.C. ruminated a moment then said 'Why don't you invite Siegfried Sassoon?' I recognised the name but Sassoon's star had fallen, if not into oblivion, into literary history. His poetry emerging from the first world war and his prose belonged to that generation. I was ashamed that I knew so little about a remarkable man but I needed a speaker. The provost gave me an address and days later I heard from Mr Sassoon that he would be pleased to come to our dinner. Of course, I informed the Lovelace Club membership how fortunate we were in having as our speaker this distinguished poet (I had investigated the anthologies) and important writer.

Siegfried Sassoon arrived and was brought to dinner after a glass of sherry in the provost's lodgings. He was courtly, with an old-fashioned politeness that I appreciated. Unfortunately, he was a little hard of hearing, which drove conversation at table in hall to an inelegant volume. He venerated Lovelace, of course, had often had reason to remember that famous 'Walls do not a prison make'. I tried to say something intelligent about poetry, and Lovelace, which, happily, I do not believe Sassoon heard. It was safer, I thought, to ask about his own work. He replied that a selection of his verse had recently been recorded by the BBC Third Programme, and, 'do you know', he said very loudly in an old man's high-pitched voice, 'that they paid me five pounds'. 'Five pounds', he repeated. Not an enormous sum even in the middle fifties. Less focused conversation followed while the next course was served and wine-glasses filled again before we adjourned to drink port and perhaps coffee.

The club reassembled in the rooms of a member large enough to accommodate and seat us all. We turned to the study of letters by my thanking our distinguished guest for his presence and inviting him to speak unless he preferred taking a question from the floor. He said he would be happy to take a question. One of our better read members asked for an opinion on modern writers and his preference. While Sassoon paused we speculated on which writer he would choose: Graham Greene or perhaps even Henry Green, if not Evelyn Waugh, or Max Beerbohm or conceivably G.K. Chesterton, obviously not a Mitford. The extended pause ended with a convincing: 'George Meredith'. We were treated to a long, thoughtful, admiring critique of George Meredith's writing, which I think few of us had read. No questions followed and the slightly awkward silence was finally broken by an American voice from the back of the room. Our only published poet, albeit an ultra-slim volume, had been elected a member for that reason; he was not in other respects what we thought of as culturally sophisticated.

'Say, Mr Sassoon', he beamed rather loudly with a pronounced mid-west accent, 'did your parents like Wagner?' Embarrassed silence clotted the room. I looked at Siegfried Sassoon, to see his reaction and was trying desperately to think of something witty, when he turned towards the speaker and in his high-pitched voice said: 'As a matter of fact, they did. Yes.' That was why he was called Siegfried. Everybody smiled. I was able to thank Mr Sassoon warmly for having come and for being so frank; we looked forward to listening to his poems on the Third Programme.

The following term I invited Auden. I think he simply enjoyed a congenial evening smoking in the company of young men, he had no intention of conducting a poetry seminar. It was all quite civilised but deposited no literary sediment. The most vivid memory of the great poet in person was his incredibly wrinkled skin. Many years later I read a comment on Auden attributed to John Hockney: 'God knows what his balls must look like.'

Term-time was often more interesting than being on vacation but not exclusively. Despite limited funds there were different experiences to be had when on holiday. A Franciscan brother, always correctly habited, haunted certain Oxford colleges, including Worcester, to generate awareness of his friary if not precisely to convert. He invited me to stay at Cerne Abbas; there would be nothing to pay. Easter approached, I had no other commitment, and the prospect of experiencing Easter in a monastic establishment became tempting.

I hitch-hiked to Dorset without undue difficulty and only when I reached the countryside nearing Cerne Abbas did I find myself deposited on a country lane with little or no traffic. It was not raining. I let my mind wander while I looked at the pleasing view of rolling fields when an old Morris Minor bumbled round the bend. It slowed down. The driver leant across and looked me over before asking where I was headed. And I knew instantly who the driver was. His distinctly recognisable picture had been in all the newspapers, a doctor accused of murdering several patients. I had to stop myself saying 'Dr Bodkin Adams, I presume'. His deceased patients had all been women but I did hesitate for a second before accepting the offer of a lift. He revealed nothing newsworthy as he drove us comfortably down the middle of the lane before delivering me without incident near the friary.

Easter with the Franciscans was a curious experience, less monastic than being in a real monastery. The brothers going about their routine business paid little attention to the visitor, did not engage in theological discussion much less casual conversation, stopping only for silent meals with scriptural reading and for religious observances. Good Friday culminated in all-pervasive silence. No words spoken, no sound, little or no movement, neither rain nor wind, a curious stillness settled heavily until Saturday midnight approached auguring the Easter liturgy. Easter arrived with the mass lighting of candles, lights everywhere and the choral singing of anthems. That spirit of light continued after the service into the dining hall where the risen Christ was hospitably received and we broke the fast in celebration. But I departed Cerne Abbas untouched by real religious emotion. A friary is not the same as a contemplative monastic order and Franciscans have a respected reputation for the practical good work they do among people. Easter in a Cistercian abbey might have moved me more.

I returned to the familiar religion of Worcester College. Members of the college were required to attend at least one service on Sundays, whether the Holy Communion, Matins or Evensong, and had to sign the relevant sheet. Attendance was predicated less on religious faith than on respect for England's interpretation of a Christian's conduct. It bolstered my developing conviction that the church had a crucial role in bringing members of the community together not only at key moments in life, baptism after birth, marriage and death, but to voice commitment to shared values while absorbing the rich, inspirational language of the Bible's Authorised King James version and the Book of Common Prayer. Worcester under J.C.Masterman reinforced the ethos of The Church of England as part of English social being. The provost, who was not himself what would be described as a religious person, always came to sit in his stall, which was wittily engraved 'God', the culminating word of the *Te Deum* as planningly carved on pew-ends round the chapel.

Christianity, of the non-demonstrative variety, was an unquestioned element in my own life. Both at home, my preparatory school and at St Paul's, Christianity was taken for granted; we absorbed the language of the prayer book and knew the hymns by heart. The Church of England from the time of the Reformation and through the turbulence of eighteenth and nineteenth century rethinking had evolved in a way I found congenial, enfolding high, middle/broad and low. It encompassed an Anglo-Catholic wing that differed little from Rome except in recognition of the papacy. At Oxford you could sniff the incense when passing St Mary Mags, beside the martyrs' memorial, while in St Aldate's, the protestant wing prevailed and you were liable to face Billy Grahamish inquisition. Between those extremes the city had a range of churches and college chapels, many with superb choirs, where the liturgy and language remained staunchly traditional C of E. The interlude in Denmark, to me it felt in many ways as an interlude, had not undermined my affinity for the Anglican church. The liturgy of the Church of Denmark was relatively similar and even church structure, though the hymns, sung seated, lacked vigour. The year in America reinforced my sense of belonging to the Anglican/Episcopal denomination.

Oxford had more than met my expectations. I had wanted so much to go up to Oxford and made considerable efforts to get there. It had been a most enjoyable experience, I had made a range of friends, been to innumerable parties, taken an active part in a wide range of activities and absorbed a huge amount of life-relevant learning. I had benefitted from exposure to highly educated and intelligent minds, been stimulated by challenging argument and learnt from those with interests other than mine. I rowed, in a lesser eight, for my college and fenced for the university to Assassins colours. But it was as if the target had been the Oxford experience not the degree course. I had done too little academic work, taken advantage of an indolent supervisor. I was examined for the B.Litt and the research degree was awarded, mainly for effort, I think. It was pleasing to put behind me a project of which I was not proud. I opted for the college grace rather than attend the ceremonial degree conferral in the Sheldonian. Career prospects remained vague; it was far from certain that I would begin qualifying for the academic-clerical post in one of the ancient universities to which I aspired, but that was still my ambition.

I had gravitated this close to being ordained almost by accident. No, that is not true. My father was a clergyman and like many children the only career of which I had meaningful knowledge was my father's. For centuries boys, and especially eldest sons, followed in their father's footsteps, not only when inheriting a title and estate but in the professions and trades. It seemed natural for my career to follow my father's, the more so after I considered the alternatives, which of course I did. This was long before freedom of choice became fashionable with today's bewildering parade of options assembled before graduates.

The expectations of the time were limited and the realistic alternatives in my world relatively few. I had some exposure to diplomacy from my parents' time in London. It attracted me but in that era a career in Britain's foreign office was closed to those not British-born and I did not fancy myself as a Danish diplomat, though my old High Master had once suggested that I might like to become Denmark's ambassador to the Court of St James'. The law I knew little about. Solicitors dealt with boring, routine legal business; being a barrister sounded more interesting – I liked the theatrical aspects – but it was understood that you had to have money behind you to be called to the bar. Medicine had seemed a possibility only when I first matriculated. School-mastering was for those with modest ambition. University appointments were another story and I aimed at a college chaplaincy with the opportunity to further my studies in the history and philosophy of religion.

6 Theology, Heidelberg and beyond

I WAS ADMITTED TO RIPON HALL, the theological college, on Boar's Hill at the edge of Oxford, in 1956, and spent a disproportionate amount of time bicycling down and back up. Many friends were still in residence and I enjoyed their company better than that of earnest-minded fellow students at Ripon Hall, almost all older than me. One exception was a graduate student on a short exchange from Heidelberg. Far from the stereotypical German he had a great sense of fun, enjoyed playing croquet after dinner, when it was not raining, or sauntering to the pub.

Gunther was committed to the ecumenical movement, of which I had some knowledge from my father, and we discussed progressive Christian thinking. We both admired Dietrich Bonhoeffer's brave stance against Hitler and sought to grasp the meaning of his 'religionless Christianity'. We explored the ideas shortly to find expression in Bishop Robinson's *Honest to God* and more. I also pestered Gunther to describe Heidelberg's duelling fraternities, but he was not a member; like many of the postwar generation he preferred to put behind him reminders of German history and its militarist traditions. Instead he told me of the ecumenical *Studentenwohnheim*, where he lived in the shadow of the castle and the *Kneipe* nearby where students gathered to drink and sing. Then one day he announced having heard from the principal that they might have a short-stay place for me. To my delight the Oxford authorities agreed in 1957 to my absence for study abroad.

The *studentenwohnheim* followed a policy that foreign students in their first semester were assigned a room to be shared with a German. My room-mate was an ultra correct Bremenite who addressed me as 'Sie' and 'Herr'. Every day began with '*Guten morgen, Herr Jensen, und haben Sie gut geschlafen?*' till just before my departure when he proposed solemnly that we call each other '*du*', he, he said, was 'Andreas'. Herr Jung respected my space as fully as he assumed my respect for his. I was not included when a couple of his friends came in to sing part-songs by candlelight – as well given my level of musicality. It was fascinating to experience such different formality, which had already challenged me with a different twist almost immediately on arriving in Heidelberg.

Before my departure from England I had called on my old tutor and found him still saying goodbye to someone. He introduced me; the man had a German-sounding name. I said that it just happened that I was about to spend time in Heidelberg. He smiled, what a fine coincidence, his family lived nearby in Mannheim, and although he himself would be travelling he was sure the family would wish to invite me. He asked for my address. Only two weeks after coming I received a formal invitation, engraved, on card, from Herr und Frau von Schimmelpfennig to a dinner-dance.

Dress was not specified as it would normally have been on a similar English invitation, where for dinner and dancing this could be white tie. I had not brought a tail-coat with me so settled for my dinner-jacket and black tie. Having been briefed on etiquette by Gunther I bought a bouquet of roses, the stems in odd number, and flourishing fifteen prime roses caught the train to Mannheim. I was greeted warmly, Frau v. Schimmelpfennig thanked me profusely for the roses and looking me appreciatively over said how elegant was Herr Jensen aus Oxford, 'The English are so formal' she added ushering me into a large drawing-room filled with young people. Every man wore a dark blue suit, white shirt and grey tie. Comparative formality became more apparent when we danced. I danced according to Oxford fashion of the time, relaxed and close. The young Germans, without exception, danced conventionally at arm's length as from an older dancing school.

Among the young women I found one who spoke a little English, helpful since I had next to no German. Why had I come to Heidelberg, she wanted to know. Since I had fenced at school and fenced for Oxford I was fascinated by the duelling fraternities, of which I had heard – seemed a plausible response and it scored a bullseye. Her father was an old Corps member and proud of it.

An invitation to dinner arrived from the Freiherr to his gloomily imposing house overlooking the Neckar. He spoke even less English than his daughter and, unlike her, was far from English friendly. For a moment he reminded me of a caricature by Groscz, his cheek and brow incised with highly visible mensur scarring. Enhanced by the stage set of dark and heavy Biedermeier furniture he exuded a powerful sense of regret for a more glorious past and the tragedy of a lost war. But he told me, through his daughter's interpretation, about the corporation to which he was honoured to belong, the Saxo-Borussia. It might be possible, he intimated, for me to join the undergraduate members at the Seppl tavern for lunch one day.

Zum Seppl I had noticed near the touristy Roter Ochsen. There Gunther and I had already been, an ancient student inn liberally decorated with fading photographs of duelling fraternities, much-used pewter and suspended from the heavily initial-engraved ceiling great drinking horns. An indifferent pianist banged out platitudinous melodies, the only words repeatedly audible above the hubbub were '*Wer soll jetzt bezahlen, wer hat so viel Geld?*' A legitimate question I thought one evening as we sat surrounded by beer wallowing students until a couple of wine-drinking tourists joined our table to raise the tone.

A well turned out man in his thirties and his attractive girl, speaking good German, enquired whether we were from the university and learning that I was a foreigner asked how I enjoyed it. We talked. When the woman realised that I was originally from Scandinavia said she had been to Norway. After an awkward pause it transpired that she had gone to place flowers on the grave of her brother killed while fighting with German forces. But, she continued very softly, no Norwegian taxi-driver would take her to the German war cemetery. At that the boy-friend banged the table, to his girl-friend's obvious embarrassment, and loudly insisted '*Man muss vergessen*'. Back at the *studentenwohnheim* an elderly English theology professor was spending six months in Germany in the hope of coming to Christian terms after the death of both his sons in the war.

At Seppl the only evidence of fighting unforgotten was on the walls in the multiple photographs of a duelling fraternity, uniform items including the student caps once widely worn but no longer in fashion and token weaponry, all bearing the insignia and colours associated with the Saxo-Borussia. The Corps Saxo-Borussia, it emerged, was socially prestigious and had been influential – Paddy Leigh Fermor described it as Heidelberg's Bullingdon and its members as Prussia's and Saxony's haughtiest. It was prosecuted by the Nazis and dissolved in 1935 but proudly recreated in 1952. I was again introduced as 'Herr Jensen aus Oxford', that becoming the standard introduction to which I had not the slightest objection provided nobody felt reminded of *The Great Gatsby*. Lacking German limited my conversation but one of those present spoke reasonable English and we enjoyed talking.

On leaving he invited me to a small party and since I did not know even his name, much less his address, I asked him to write it on a scrap of paper. It read Pr R z Lippe, and Prince Rudolf became a friend. He had already earned his mensur, with contemporary fashion repositioning the scar from high visibility cheek to being discreetly hair-covered. At the impressive Corpshaus–

Riesenstein, I was introduced to novice members of the Saxo-Borussia. Old members maintained the premises in style. A liveried man-servant opened the door when I arrived, took my jacket and helped me into a superbly be-frogged hussar-like coat before guiding me to a panelled room where eight or nine similarly clad sat around a heavy refectory table laden under pint beer-mugs of cut glass with ornate armorial lids. The novice master greeted me formally.

The moment I was seated a jug of beer appeared before me. The table, which I was admiring, was deeply incised following youthful practice but the quality of carving had nothing schoolboyish about it. The lettering was exquisite and ornamentation in perfect taste and I recognised several names of eminent Germans. Suddenly: 'Moltke', I thought that was how it sounded, when the novice master commanded, 'Singt vor nummer sieben und dreisig'. The novice leapt to his feet and began to sing number thirty-seven in the Corps songbook. 'Nein, gehts nicht. Noch einmal.' More singing orders followed and much more drinking.

Fencing had prompted my interest in Heidelberg's fraternities, but fencing as sport bore little resemblance to Corps practice. Even duelling was a misleading description. The procedure followed meticulous rules: the 'duellers' stood just under two swords length apart, padded against danger to vital organs, veins and arteries but leaving exposed aspects of the face. The sabres, with elaborate basket guards, were razor sharpened at the point (no foil buttons here) and the fight consisted not of footwork but of subtle wrist movement aimed at slashing the opponent's brow, cheek or chin deeply enough to achieve scarring, which was further ensured by rubbing in salt.

The challenge was not to wince, to endure pain without showing it. The visible evidence of higher education and social preferment was then worn for life. This was a class rite. Both the sabre handling techniques and the ritual in general involved training and practice spaced over one semester; only in the semester following could the new member prove himself and complete the novitiate. My one term in Heidelberg was too short. But as Christmas approached the Corps held a party. Members young and old were invited and a few daughters or sisters, no other women were admitted.

I was a special guest and seated beside a distinguished officer who had campaigned in north Africa under Rommel. My German was by now adequate to understanding his description of desert warfare. He reminisced about battles fought as if it had been a match between rival schools; he considered the English worthy rivals, opponents who respected the rules of military engagement. Only speeches interrupted his further rumination, speeches in high German that I was working with limited success to interpret until I heard my name. Herr Jensen aus Oxford had been a much appreciated guest member. In token of that appreciation the Corps wished to honour me with a presentation *Weinzipfel*, the regency's fob-chain elegantly adapted for contemporary wear. I was awarded a narrow strap of heavy silk in Saxo-Borussia colours with fastenings in silver and set with clasps bearing the Corps cipher, and engraved with a dedication to *'seiner lieben Erik Jensen'*. A more charming memento of Heidelberg I could not have wished.

Come from Heidelberg for my parents' silver wedding banquet

Back in Oxford the General Ordination Examination posed little challenge and I survived the ensuing interviews. Although I did not envisage life as a parish priest the beginning of any clerical career, also in higher education, normally entailed a curacy. I had reconnoitred a couple of curate-seeking parishes where the incumbent failed to appeal before being interviewed by the rector of St Mary Abbot's, parish church of the heart of Kensington, and was awaiting confirmation of an appointment with the suffragan bishop.

I still bicycled occasionally down Boar's Hill to see old friends and for special events. A talk about Albert Schweitzer, his beliefs and work, was being given at Pusey House and Schweitzer had become something of a role model for me. I respected his academic writings as a theologian, which I had studied at Harvard, I admired his musical talents – his art form – and I was deeply impressed by his commitment to humanitarian work among Africans. I arrived slightly late, having been diverted en route, and missed the beginning but heard enough to realise that this was of serious interest.

I wrote immediately to the principal to enquire whether the text was being made available. It was not, he replied, but there would be a summary, which he could give me if I would like to come to lunch later that week. I had never met Father Maycock although he was known to some of my friends. When I asked about him everything seemed predictable, much as one would expect of an Anglican academic, bar one thing. He had spent four years in Borneo. Lunch passed amicably enough with a light peppering of clerical wit. The only serious conversation related to my research, my interest in comparative religion, and this was not prolonged. Maycock then invited me to his study where he would give me the notes from the talk about Schweitzer. Schweitzer's jungle hospital in west Africa seemed extremely remote as we sat drinking coffee in that classical Oxford setting. So remote it somehow brought Borneo to mind.

'I have heard, Father Maycock, that you spent years in Borneo' I asked with the hint of a question mark, it seemed hardly plausible. 'As a matter of fact, I did, before the war', he replied without elaborating, nothing about orang-utan, head-hunters, Dyak belles or braves, or his personal experience, why, as I later learned, he left with no regrets and unregretted. 'Are you interested?' I said it sounded unusual. Only as I was leaving did Maycock mention that the bishop of Borneo was over for the Lambeth Conference and would be in Oxford that weekend. Would I like to come by for a glass of sherry?

The bishop of Borneo was a handsome man, with a slightly provocative habit of fingering his pectoral cross. He said he had heard from Father Maycock of my interest in comparative religion. I could not resist provoking him a little. I said that I had been studying the relationship between religion and the economy in simple societies and wondered why missionaries sometimes ignored the implications of conversion for economic behaviour and vice versa. 'Ah, but that isn't true', he said, and went on to explain that the church was well aware of the complex relationship between people's religion and other aspects of social life. The clergy, however, were rarely qualified to pursue this academically and the majority did not see their vocation in that light. We finished drinking our sherry while we talked round the subject for a minute or two before he stopped, looked me straight in the eye and said: 'If you feel so strongly about this why don't you do some work in Borneo?' He thought there might be a berth available that autumn of 1958. I was unsure how to respond. It sounded exciting, but. The bishop was not about to let me off the hook. I would have to agree to a three-year contract and would be remunerated like clergy in the diocese. He would ensure that I could carry out research in an appropriate district, before adding that he would count on me for occasional help.

My friends thought I was out of my mind, my brother expected me to have second thoughts, my mother worried. I felt deceived when the bishop wrote that a berth would not, after all, be available that autumn and he proposed that before sailing I spend some time with a priest who had served in Sarawak for years and spoke a local language. The priest was vicar of a modest parish in rural Essex. Not as I had planned but by then other options had been abandoned. I spent nine months with Father Sparrow. His affection for the people of Sarawak was real and he retained impressive command of spoken Iban, but he was not a natural language teacher and lacked a linguist's ability to explain the very different syntax and grammar, and there were no books on the subject. As a learning method he suggested we recite Matins daily in Iban; the office had been translated and he gave me a copy of the text. Since he was somewhat deaf my Iban rendition of the responses could have been any language by the time they had crossed the aisle.

Long before the days of affordable air travel the journey east in 1959 was by sea. Elegant, classified, unhurried, and a geography lesson. The climate changed and the countryside, the appearance of the people and how they behaved. From the classical Christian cultures of Europe, witnessed from Gibraltar to Malta, and the pervasive influence of Greece, we approached the Suez canal and the Arab Islamic world. Along the canal we surveyed the seemingly endless sands, the occasional ass plodding round a water pump's treadmill and a camel or two. Aden was hot and humid before we departed the Islamic middle east and crossed the ocean towards the Indian subcontinent and Sri Lanka. Complexions altered and dress. And they changed again when twenty days out of the port of London we docked in Singapore.

Lying in the roads was an antiquated vessel of the Straits Shipping Company and the following afternoon, as dusk was about to fall, a lighter navigated me between the massive hulls of ships at anchor to where a rope ladder over the side enabled me to clamber aboard the *Rajah Brooke*. Straits Steamship had the reputation of carrying passengers and cockroaches in equal quantity but first-class passengers banished such awkward co-travellers as best they could with generous measures of gin. Forty-eight hours after sailing from Singapore we snaked our way cautiously up the Sarawak river to Kuching, following the same trajectory as James Brooke a century earlier, prior to becoming the first rajah. The deck passengers came volubly to life as they assembled their merchandise, counting the chicks that had been planned to hatch at this moment, and muscled ashore the moment we docked.

7 Sarawak, to the longhouses

OLD SARAWAK had enormous charm and I was immediately taken by the beauty of the river, the original court house and facing it across the water the Astana. The Astana was the palace where Brooke rajahs had lived royally before it became the governor's residence when Sarawak was made a crown colony after the second war. In the relative cool of the evening after my arrival I wandered past shophouses lining the streets, all built to the same plan with the shop below and storage and accommodation behind and above. The upper storey projected making a covered walkway, the five-foot way, in front. Enticing smells came from India street where they sold spices and products from the subcontinent.

Every street had its distinctive odour. From the open market came the smell of cooking and noise. I found a place to sit. And observed my cook hacking and chopping with his vicious-looking knife. Behind his hissing stove was an unlit area from which he produced the wherewithal to prepare remarkably good food. The dim lighting masked the rubbish lying about, discarded newspaper, straws and unidentifiable bits and pieces through which I detected a rat in search of anything edible. Odour from the open drains was drenched away when it suddenly poured with rain. We were hustled under cover, such tin-roofing as there was, while the rain pelted the corrugated iron, cleared the air and smells with it. As abruptly as it had begun it stopped. A cannon boomed loudly. No one reacted or seemed alarmed; I learnt that this was a custom derived from the Brooke raj: the rajah could be approached by any Sarawakian until eight o'clock when he dined, as announced by the cannon.

Next day I had a meeting with the bishop to discuss arrangements: where I was to be based, how I would travel and what he expected of me. Sarawak had only fifteen miles of surfaced road and it did not lead even that little way towards Simanggang, from where I was to depart into the remote interior. Travel was on foot or by boat. It had been arranged, the bishop said, that a government launch would deposit me at Sebuyau, a small bazaar near the mouth of the Sarawak river. Passing Chinese trading launches took on merchandise and the occasional passenger. I was expected to find a launch destined for Simanggang and make my way up the great Batang Lupar river. The river was famous for its tidal bore, the bore that nearly drowned Somerset Maugham to the regret of those expatriates whose personal indiscretions provided material for his colourful short stories. The helmsman, with much clanking of ancient chains, manoeuvred us away from hidden sandbanks and submerged obstacles eventually to arrive at Simanggang. A seaman leapt into the water with a line to the wharf and we were moored just before the bore thundered up-river.

On the outskirts of Simanggang the Anglican mission had a school and church. The priest-in-charge was to help with arrangements for my onward journey. Father Turner was preoccupied with more serious ecclesiastical business. He had been requested to arrange Christian burial for the remains of a white man and a local woman, both headless. He demurred: heads or no heads could he be sure that they had been married according to Christian rites? Later I heard from the district officer whose bodies they were. The man, Arundel, had been a senior administrative officer and magistrate of the last rajah's and had sentenced an up-river Iban for a brutal killing. Although he urged clemency the rajah only deferred the death sentence. At the Japanese invasion Arundel, who spoke fluent Iban and whose wife was Iban, escaped to the remote interior where he felt secure among friendly Iban. But the Japanese, when they discovered the evasion, released the killer from prison and promised to revoke his death-sentence provided he brought back the heads of Arundel and his wife. Father Turner was persuaded to give what remained Christian burial. With respect to my arrangements he introduced a senior school-boy from the Undup who directed me to where I could find an outboard driver familiar with the river.

For days and days it rained. The northeast monsoon, I was told, had broken. The outboard driver explained that with this much rain the turbulent Undup became not navigable. Although it was still raining lightly when towards the end of the week I presented myself in the early morning he decided to set off. Under sheets of plastic and defended by oil-paper umbrellas we embarked. The downpour began to ease as we approached the Undup, a major tributary of the Batang Lupar, and the sun broke through while we angled into the mouth of the river. Muddy banks sloped away on both sides and behind them a mass of vegetation fronted tall trees. I was looking about me, attempting to dry off in the sunshine, and marvelling at all I saw. Suddenly on the bank no distance away I faced my living introduction to the rain forest world. A huge crocodile lay its great mouth expectantly wide open to display the finest array of butchering teeth. The outboard-driver revved the engine. The crocodile snapped shut its jaws and, with extraordinary agility and speed disappeared down into the river. They do not like the noise of outboard engines, the driver explained, while I removed my hand from beyond the gunwale and wondered where in the murky water the crocodile was lying in wait.

We made our way laboriously up-river through shallows, where the longboat had to be dragged across rapids and man-handled over a waterfall. After eight hours of squatting on wooden slats my legs ached and I stared expectantly round every bend till the driver announced Batu Lintang when an embankment appeared in the distance through the overhanging trees. A small crowd, assembled for the evening bath, awaited the longboat from Simanggang in expectation of news and merchandise. The driver cut out the engine the moment we bumped against a notched log forming a ladder up from the water's edge. The noise of frogs croaking in all keys and the din of cicadas trumpeted my arrival as I uncrumpled my stiff-jointed legs, tottered, and attempted to find a foothold on the slimy log only to begin slipping. A gentle hand preserved me from falling and Nuli, headmaster of the new Batu Lintang school, escorted me firmly to the top. 'You would like to drink?' he asked in English, 'Would you like beer?' I accepted gratefully and we entered Chakong's shophouse.

Chakong was a Chinese whose father had married an Iban and he was well-accepted. In an inner corner we sat at a marble-topped table, on which Chakong placed two large bottles of Anchor beer. Nuli tapped the top with an opener and froth spewed wildly when the cap came off. We drank warm beer enthusiastically while Nuli told me that two senior schoolboys had been designated to help organise my camp-bed in the hut available for me and get my pressure-lamp up and functioning. After 'taking my bath' he invited me to 'take my dinner' with him; he lived in simple quarters on the upper floor of the school, which was close by. When I enquired where I should bathe he replied 'the Undup river' as if this was self-evident.

Nuli was as able as he was generous. He had been chosen for a pioneer training programme of teachers for rural areas, had learnt some English in the process and was an excellent example for the community in adapting to the economic and social changes it faced. He considered himself a Christian but was unfailingly respectful of his father, Sampar, the distinguished headman of a longhouse at the head of the river, and Sampar followed the traditional religion scrupulously. In less than two months it would be Christmas and Nuli asked me to celebrate at his father's longhouse. I concentrated hard on acquiring more of the language, as might be appreciated in a guest. Christmas at Rumah Sampar was unlike any Christmas I had experienced but as festive, replete with good will, good drink and good food, as portrayed in any 'God rest you merry gentlemen' image. We drank copiously of the Iban's own tuak, rice beer made by fermenting glutinous rice, feasted on roast wild boar and other dishes, accompanied by much lively talk, laughter and Iban dances. A Christian Christmas was observed while Iban rituals were to be celebrated later according to their liturgical calendar, and I would be a welcome observer.

Traditional Iban were committed to their ancestors' way of life. Every stage in the rice planting cycle demanded rites, and these were meticulously observed. Failure to do so had consequences for the harvest, it was believed. The agricultural year began with what was also the preceding year's harvest festival, and a major feast, to which relatives and friends from other houses were also invited. Sacrificial offerings, a pig, a fowl and important items of food and chewing ingredients, were seriously, though not too solemnly, prepared for the gods, and accompanied by invocations. Drinking and eating, talk and laughter, traditional dances, animated the longhouse, with drunkenness signifying a good party. Precious handwoven *pua* (ceremonial cloths rather than blankets as they were misleadingly translated) served as frontal to a dignified shrine. Round it a lemambang bard, accompanied by two acolytes, marched rhythmically pounding his staff while intoning a many-hour long prayer to the principal deities whose presence and blessing were sought to assure an ample harvest.

Lesser rites took place at the farm, before dibbling and planting, during growth, prior to harvesting and when the harvested rice was carried home. The sacred seed rice, the *padi pun*, was treated throughout with the utmost respect, as if it had human sensitivities. The Iban believed that the gods, more specifically Pulang Gana, had revealed to them the mysteries necessary to successful rice cultivation and Senglang Burong the interpretation of certain bird calls perceived as conveying supernatural guidance. Though their beliefs encompassed other aspects of life, health, family, the longhouse community and once upon a time head-hunting, the hill rice cult dominated.

For centuries throughout their remembered history the Iban had followed a pattern of entering new rain forest, felling trees, clearing undergrowth and burning before planting rice. They built a longhouse close to the river, which served as source of water, for bathing, for fishing and communication. Despite the hilly terrain, with scorching sunshine and torrential rain leaching the soil, the accessible land area, nourished by potash, could be expected to deliver

Longhouse exterior and interior

Fetching water from the river

Farms in Sarawak interior

65

adequate harvests for up to fifteen years. When harvests declined the Iban moved on and repeated the cycle elsewhere, *pindah*, they called it. Pindah caused problems only when the Iban sought to occupy forest inhabited by less assertive tribes, but Sarawak had vast areas in reserve. The rajah's eventual success in suppressing head-hunting, increasingly effective control of deadly disease epidemics combined with the natural increase in population began to make ever greater demands on access to unexploited jungle while at the same time concern for timber and forest conservation, combined with policies to encourage a settled population and increased cultivation of cash crops like rubber and pepper, rural schooling, improved communication and health services all militated against recurrent displacement.

Sampar observed the traditional rites scrupulously and was rewarded with generous harvests. He was also an intelligent man aware of changes in the world about him. He realised that his three sons might not have the cultivable acreage necessary to feed their families in the upper Undup, let alone a further batch of grandchildren, He witnessed several local Iban, who had ventured into service as tracker-soldiers, return with broadened experience and new ideas. Since the rajah's time the Undup had provided recruits for the Sarawak Rangers and later to serve as tracker-soldiers during the Malayan emergency. A handful of others had some education at the mission school in Simanggang. Education provided by mission schools opened the young Iban's mind, exposing him to new ways of earning a living including unfamiliar crops like rubber which could provide a valuable source of cash income. But it also undermined faith in bird omens and sacrificial offerings to the old gods and sowed the idea of Christianity.

Sampar supported his son Nuli when he went away for schooling and was eventually chosen for teacher training. Teachers assigned to remote areas were expected to provide leadership and foster understanding of improved agriculture. Nuli set a fine example by planting high-yielding rubber saplings and advising on other crops. Shifting hill rice cultivation was not readily compatible with these. Its land requirement involved access to ever new areas of unexploited forest imposing constant migration, the Iban pindah, while population growth adding to the acreage exploited gave the leached jungle soils ever less time to recover. Pindah imposed a further sacrifice when it meant abandoning the time and effort invested in rubber trees, a price the Iban became increasingly loath to pay. The Undup Iban were fortunate in having sufficient territory to smooth the transition and, not least, in having leaders with the foresight to guide their people. Nuli took the lead, as a Christian.

Christianity helped ease the passage to a settled way of life from traditional cultivation and pindah. It filled the space left when the sequence of rites related to hill rice culture no longer absorbed the Iban but without unduly disrupting the old habits and longhouse living. Islam was the region's other proseletising religion. Converting to Islam was uncomplicated, not least because most Iban men were already circumcised, but involved a radical change of life-style. The convert was required to take a Muslim name and expected to wear clothing, such as the Malays wore, including their distinctive headgear. It was described in Iban, not as 'masok Islam' but 'masok Melayu', becoming Malay. This conferred a new identity, which was no longer Iban. Christianity on the other hand had the advantage of permitting the eating of pork, an Iban favourite, drinking, if not officially inebriation, and imposed no dress rules or obligatory change of name. It came associated with progress through education and the speaking of English but your identity remained indubitably Iban.

The bishop underwrote my research project but counted on me, he repeated, to help the diocese in various ways. The first was to design the cover of a new diocesan magazine and illustrate points in the text; he had been told – by whom? – that I was good at drawing. For the cover I drew the new cathedral, recently consecrated, surrounded by appropriate lettering in English, Chinese and Iban. The illustrations were more challenging since the points to be illustrated nearly all related to sexual morality. This was still the nineteen-fifties and the bishop subscribed to his inherited Victorian code, as officially propagated by the Church of England, which proscribed premarital sexual relations, cohabitation without marriage, and remarriage after divorce.

The Iban, I was learning, had their own somewhat different sexual morality, well adapted to longhouse living. They were not promiscuous and intolerant of indiscriminate sexuality. But a young man and woman could be alone together in only one way, and their practice of courting, ngayap, did permit a degree of intimacy. The young man, attracted by a girl, who had reciprocated an interest, was expected to climb at night the wall into the girl's family room where, as a nubile young woman, she had her own space and mosquito-net. If she fancied him she allowed him into the net where they were able to converse softly and touch each other. Intercourse commonly followed after one or more follow-up visits unless, meanwhile, the girl had decided not to pursue the relationship in which case the man had no option but to disappear and knew he would not be welcome back in that family room. Father and mother sleeping nearby were fully aware of the visit but intervened only if their daughter indicated.

After repeated visits it was not unusual to establish the man's intentions.

If 'serious' the parents of boy and girl met to discuss with which family the couple should reside. Any sign of pregnancy was welcome. The young Iban had neither cinema nor dance-hall, nor any other place in which to become acquainted with each other and be alone together. Ngayap worked well. But it sanctioned pre-marital intimacy contrary to church teaching although, as it happened, it was close to the norms beginning to emerge in post-pill Europe.

Co-habitation without marriage was harder to condemn because the Iban considered as married any couple that had been living together for a week or more. The church, of course, meant marriage solemnised in a Christian rite. Remarriage after divorce was impossible to censure: it provided the solution when a couple was childless. The Iban depended on children to support them in old age. Unless they could adopt the child of a relative, a couple without children was obliged to divorce and remarry. In such circumstances divorce was uncomplicated. Divorce when there were children was far less straightforward and not common. I found the Iban code eminently sensible and expressing a morality of which I could not bring myself to disapprove. I did little pen and ink sketches of different Iban heads and shoulders for the bishop to decorate the injunctions in his pamphlet, wishing I could add a light disclaimer. I was pleased that the printed copies, for distribution, never reached me.

My help in propagating Christianity, as Nuli suggested, was another matter. I enjoyed updating parables from first century Israel into the Iban world, making them locally intelligible. The all-pervading importance of sheep and the 'good shepherd' in Christian works posed a real problem for people who had never seen or had any exposure to sheep. Pigs they knew all about and cared for but pigs were not an acceptable alternative. No other animal, except perhaps the dog, suggested itself. On the other hand references to fish, fishing and fisher of men were easy to transpose. The good Samaritan could become the good Chinese who went out of his way to help an Iban. One god differed from several deities in Iban religion but was not difficult to grasp; the trinity I interpreted as the one god manifested differently – half-heresy, I knew, but it made the belief readily accessible. Virgin birth was not a special stumbling-block, they half believed it.

I was invited to visit most of the longhouses within some two hours walking distance. My coming provided a pretext for killing a chicken and bringing out the gongs after supper for music and a dance. Later, sitting on straw-mats by the dim light of tapers, we relaxed as the Iban gathered round for the customary *berandau*, general conversation. Berandau was an occasion to exchange news and provided the day's entertainment, which a visitor made particularly interesting. I was asked all manner of questions, about my journey to the Undup and, more personal, about my family and why I was not married if my younger brother was and how much I earned. Since I was Christian – they assumed that all white men were – could I also tell them about it. My command of Iban was sorely stretched but gradually improved with repeated stretching. I endeavoured to describe core elements of Christian belief and practice, drawing on my parable transpositions and what I believed to be the essence of Christian living. Discussion continued sometimes for hours. The more thoughtful Iban were searching for an alternative to the inherited religion as they perceived that becoming less relevant to their daily existence. What they sought was for the whole community. In traditional belief individual conduct had implications for the community: the longhouse was liable to suffer for any one person's non-observance of the appropriate rites. This applied, therefore, to individual conversion. The longhouse, the community, would have to become Christian, not the isolated individual, much as occurred in the early history of Christianity in much of Europe.

I worked closely with Nuli on practical school-based projects with which he sympathised. With me as lead digger we created an extensive and productive model vegetable garden; fishponds were encouraged but the area round the school was unsuitable. Once a week I held an informal clinic at which I dispensed Aspirin from the enormous jar I had purchased in London, sulphaguanadine badgered from the medical department, and applied gentian violet as needed while trying to inculcate notions of hygiene.

More contentious was my ambition to introduce an unfamiliar item to the school curriculum: I proposed that classes, voluntary classes, be given in Iban weaving. In the longhouses I had been shown beautiful examples of traditional weaving, *pua*. As I knew from my stay at Sampar's longhouse, Pua were greatly prized as works of art and displayed on ceremonial occasions; their weavers were honoured. The process demanded skill, many, many hours of work and more specifically initiation into the subtle, suggestive designs that were confidentially passed down by mother to daughter. But young girls attending school developed other interests and once the transmittal chain was broken the mysteries of weaving pua were liable to be forgotten. An elderly woman, famous for her weaving, had said she would cooperate when a small group of Iban arrived to announce that they really saw no point in having a school if the children were to be taught a traditional longhouse skill. The Iban knew how to weave pua, they sent their sons and daughters to school to learn what the white man knew, like how to make an outboard engine. Further discussion did nothing to change their conviction; the project was abandoned.

Months passed with many longhouse evenings and much talk. The season approached when *gawai* festivals were traditionally celebrated to mark the harvest and invoke the gods' blessing on the agricultural year ahead. That was when Nuli accompanied a group of leaders from several longhouses to ask whether they could become Christian. No Billy Graham gesture of individuals declaring themselves for Christ but communities accepting to practise Christianity as their religion, much as I guessed occurred before Augustine in England, Patrick in Ireland and Olaf in the north. The formalities, following instruction in the creed and knowledge of the Lord's prayer, were straightforward: baptism and to become fully incorporated in the Anglican communion confirmation by a bishop.

I wrote to the bishop asking when an episcopal visitation might be possible. On hearing the numbers involved he promised to make every effort to travel to the Undup. The weather was benign, a special boat was equipped and in an adapted part of the school premises the bishop, mitred and coped, confirmed at one, prolonged ceremony in the summer of 1960 the largest number of converts in diocesan history. Exhausted, sweat drenched, he eventually had to limit those still wishing to come forward with a promise to return. There would certainly be more, I warned the bishop, after another large longhouse community completed celebration of a final great Iban *gawai* before becoming Christian and sending their children to school.

Empadi was nearly three hours walk away, a relatively prosperous community that had recently built a fine new longhouse with high quality timber in earnest of the intention to remain in the area and develop settled agriculture. The *gawai Kenyalang* was the greatest of Iban festivals and it was celebrated in style. A great boar was ceremonially sacrificed and numerous sacrificial acts performed, exquisitely carved hornbill effigies were raised high to defy the enemy and invoke prosperity. Prayers were intoned long into the night, while the men and women of Empadi, in party dress, welcomed the guests with copious drink and their best food. For nearly three days of uninhibited merriment people feasted, danced and enjoyed this final manifestation of a way of life that might be approaching an end.

I had been invited by the headman and also by a young Iban whose case I had effectively supported in his bid for further schooling in Simanggang; he especially wanted his mother to meet me. The mother, it transpired, was a widow in straitened circumstances. She survived in a tiny room at the end of the longhouse and was largely dependent on her son's contribution. She greeted me with tears in her eyes, apologised for being unable to offer hospitality but wanted so much to tell me personally how grateful she was for all I had done for her son. She held my hands in silence for a moment then very quietly said that he was about to become Christian like others in the longhouse, but, she near whispered, she could not, she was very old and she wanted to be together with her son's father when she died. And she began crying. For several minutes I stood with her in silence before returning to noise and the crowd.

The numerous visitors brought news from all around. Most exciting were reports of an uprising among the Lemanak Iban. The Lemanak was an important tributary of the Batang Lupar between the Skrang and the Ulu Ai and on the opposite bank to the Undup and Kumpang. Iban identity was refined by naming the river valley they inhabited, where their relatives lived and within which they habitually married. In head-hunting days potential enemies occupied the next river valley, and the Iban of the valley beyond, sharing a common enemy, were loosely allied. The Lemanak Iban had an ill reputation among the Undup Iban, who seemed less than surprised that those backward, unschooled, anti-authority people had taken up arms against government.

Details were emerging that a known recalcitrant headman of the upper Lemanak, enfuriated by permission to pindah being repeatedly denied, refused to pay a token tax levied on all households and when threatened with armed police enforcement had persuaded his longhouse and neighbouring houses to resist. In 1960 they began to construct war-stockades, cleaned their shotguns and collected ammunition, and those without firearms sharpened spears and swords. Shooting was only averted at the very last moment by the intervention of a respected chief who warned that bloodshed, according to Iban belief, could have disastrous consequences for the region's fertility. The armed police expedition was withdrawn from the Lemanak but left the motive for confrontation unresolved.

How to resolve the dispute, what to do, was the first question put to me by the responsible administrative officer when I arrived in Simanggang to purchase my monthly supplies. Richards was a surviving rajah's officer, who had seen service in different parts of Sarawak but mainly among the Iban whose language he spoke fluently. He was devoted to the people of Sarawak. He had been quick to take an interest in my activities and would invite me home when I was in Simanggang. As happened on this occasion. He was not surprised that the news of the disturbance had spread. Again he asked: 'What do you think should be done?' Nobody denied that conditions in the Lemanak were deplorable, an increasing population had over-farmed the land, the soils were leached and the Iban had no other sources of income. Of course they wanted to pindah but that was no longer an option, it could not even be considered under current legislation. Richards looked at me, he waited.

With all the confidence of a twenty-six-year-old and based on my modest Undup experience I outlined a simple scheme on the community development principle of 'with the people, for the people, by the people'. A school or schools, measures leading to settled agriculture, vegetable gardening, fishponds, fruit cultivation and the planting of cash crops, to be realised by persuading the Lemanak Iban that their future and that of their children and grandchildren lay in the Lemanak, that pindah was completely out of the question. Work would have to be carried out with their own manpower and using available tools or such equipment as they knew how to operate. They would have to be convinced that this was their project in their own best interest. No large scale investment was involved, no heavy machinery to be deployed and minimal staff. Richards nodded. After a long moment's silence, he said: 'Would you do it?' I had not expected this. I had not, but it was precisely the challenge I sought, the realisation of what I believed my Christian vocation to be and true to Schweitzer's inspiring example. Had I known how extreme the Lemanak crisis was, how close to starving many people were, how poor their prospects and how bitterly resentful of government or any outside action I might have demurred, though I doubt it. I asked to think over my reply but Richards knew I was saying yes.

8 Iban revolt in the Lemanak

RICHARDS WAS RELIEVED. I was soon to learn that he had been severely criticised for failing to act in timely fashion to avert an armed uprising. He was under pressure to submit plans promptly to resolve the Lemanak problem at minimal expense and manpower deployment. No competent Iban-speaking administrative officer was available or likely to accept a three-year assignment to the notorious Lemanak. Richards was convinced my appointment would be welcomed with relief in official Kuching. The bishop, though not enthusiastic, did not object provided I accepted no increase in income.

First stage would be for me to visit the area and I was offered a longboat to deliver me to the middle Lemanak longhouse of the area chief. We set off up-river from Simanggang, passing the mouth of the Undup to the right and the Skrang on the opposite bank before turning into the Lemanak hours later. Few signs of habitation interfered with the wild undergrowth, which proliferated everywhere beneath the giant trees arching towards each other across the river. On a broken, partly submerged, branch a six-foot iguana flicked its tongue expectantly at a bloated dead pig floating down. The only sign of life till we rounded yet another bend and on the bank saw a party of Iban stodgily treading sago. They ignored us, and they wanted us to ignore them. I had not previously passed in a boat without being hailed, being asked where I was headed and often invited to a longhouse. These Iban were humiliated at having to tread sago, a measure taken most reluctantly when rice harvests failed, and they concealed their humiliation with silence.

Arrival at the chief's house was equally dispiriting. No one rushed forward to help me disembark and I was stumbling through mud, miscellaneous waste and pigs up to the longhouse when the headman appeared to greet me. That the longhouse was in poor condition was obvious without the headman himself drawing attention to it, saying as he did so that they only wanted to pindah. The area chief occupied what had once been an impressive room where great Chinese jars bore testimony to his antecedents. Little else remained of a happier past. The customary polite disclaimer when offering food 'Nadai lauk' – 'there is nothing to go with the rice', said whatever the number of side dishes, was not modesty here but a statement of fact. I was given a taste of rice with sago and a minute sliver of salt fish. This was so unlike the Iban hospitality I encountered elsewhere, and the chief knew it. It was embarrassing for a man of his status. 'We have no land left for growing rice', he said categorically, 'pindah has to be the answer.' At the general longhouse gathering afterwards the headman, more aggressively than the chief, led a chorus of pindahs. They listened to my proposals but their response never varied: the only realistic solution was pindah.

Government initiatives were as useless as the anti-Malaria campaign with DDT spraying which only made women and children ill – several women coughed obligingly – and killed the cats – no cats, you see – leading to a surge in vermin, while malaria persisted. Might they permit a school, I ventured. They saw little point since they intended moving, but they would not object provided this did not become a pretext for exacting payment. The chief agreed to my living in a rough shack outside the longhouse; it had previously housed a fighting-cock, I discovered.

The Undups showed genuine sadness at my leaving. I had lived among them for little over a year but the friendship was real. They did not approve of my moving to the Lemanak. It could be dangerous. 'If they take your head we'll raise a war-party and take theirs' was said to comfort me. Comfort was more than welcome during my early weeks among the Lemanak Iban. I visited over a dozen longhouses within an hour or two's walking distance. One refused any meeting at all and in the others long hours of endless longhouse discussion made small progress. None was interested in hygiene and health or improvements in childbirth practices, anything related to agriculture was dismissed by saying they had no land, which, of course, was why they wanted to pindah.

The three most accessible longhouses finally agreed to having a school on temporary premises. I implored the education department to waive the token fee required everywhere, but without success. It was the only means, I was told, to ensure regular attendance. Although painstakingly explained to the Iban this was certain to create problems. It did. When the new schoolmaster first reminded his pupils beforehand about the fee then sought to collect it, they refused. They refused again when he tried once more. The schoolmaster said he would request immediate reassignment unless I resolved the problem. After I had addressed the class some of the more docile children complied with one small girl bursting into tears, she had forgotten earlier to tell her parents she claimed, but the three older boys remained adamant in their refusal to pay. These boys, adolescents, although technically over-age for primary schooling, had been so keen that the age restriction was waived. They faced me brashly. I asked the oldest, standing with a cocky grin on his face, whether he had been to the recent cockfight. He had. That implied placing a bet, as he knew. I told him, and the other two adolescents, to leave the classroom and to return only when the fee was paid. They left with bad grace, embarrassed by a reprimand in public. I had done what had to be done while dreading the consequences. Outside the schoolroom a woman screamed: one moment I badgered them to attend school and the next – and she shook her fist at me.

In the longhouse that evening the mood was sombre. Nothing was said about the school until I tried explaining yet again about the fee and why it was required. No comment. Then Empajang, the father of one of the boys sent home, attacked me for humiliating his son, adding how absurd it was to pressure the Iban into schooling and then send children away. He wanted the school closed. No one else said a word. The following morning Empajang passed my shack and invited me to follow him to his farm-hut, some two hours away. I went, unsure as to his purpose.

Perched on a precipitously angled hill the hut looked down towards a swamp. Inside three naked children bustled about while their mother, squatting on a rush-mat, patted a plaintively crying baby. Boils covered the tiny body, erupting through the shaven head. Empajang spoke to his wife and she removed a black cloth, green with age, from a jar in the corner, releasing a duststorm of mosquitoes. 'Mosquitoes', she said while rummaging for a glass. She found two, opaque with grime and filled them with tuak from the jar. One she gave to her husband, the other she handed to me with her finger crooked in the glass, then noticing a drowned mosquito she wiggled in another finger to extract it. Empajang drained his glass in one swallow; I drank mine as fast as I could, it tasted sour.

He had a special *tuak* for me, Empajang said with a smirk, and reached for a bottle behind the jar. He filled my glass but not his own. He did not want any he said when I asked. This was not normal Iban practice. It was hard to decode. Iban poisoning was often psychological, predicated on fear. To accept the challenge of an ordeal was proof of resilience, of courage, of confidence: this could be the test of me and my guardian spirits. I would fail if I refused to drink. I drank the tuak. And suffered only the usual upset stomach next day. The schoolmaster was greatly relieved when I returned; he had been convinced that I was being poisoned and had already prepared his early transfer request for submission to the education department. But the big boys were back at school the following week.

Among the Iban in the chief's longhouse was a quietly spoken, more thoughtful man with whom I often had useful conversation. He was a devout adherent of traditional Iban belief and ritual, respectful of bird omens and dreams, to which he attributed the relatively better yields he obtained. But he recognized that the old religion was not entirely compatible with changes in the world around them. He supported his daughter going to school and wanted her to learn to read and write and to understand more about the ways of the white man. We enjoyed talking. One evening he said that while he and a few others might be interested in what I had to propose, the majority were not. They wanted to pindah, and only pindah. They seemed convinced that by rejecting my proposals, if necessary scaring me away, forcing me to leave the Lemanak and abandon the project, pindah would be permitted. And so long as they believed that there was nothing I could do. I did everything to persuade those who would listen that pindah was not going to be an option, but they refused to believe me.

One fine morning as I stood by the riverside wondering how to proceed I heard the beating of gongs and thump of drums grow gradually louder announcing the approach of an armada of boats. One after the other they paraded by. A wedding, I assumed. In Iban custom the bride was sometimes borne in style to the longhouse where the wedding ceremony was being held. She would sit panoplied by red flags and pennants. But no bride appeared. And I was perplexed by the great number of boats piled high with possessions. Where were these people going, I enquired. They are the Iban of Lubok Subong and they are migrating, ka pindah.

Lubok Subong was the one longhouse that had declined any meeting. I understood why. By Lemanak standards they were relatively well-off, had decided to realise all such assets as they could and use the funds to pay for transport by Chinese launches to the Fifth Division where some relatives had once settled. And deliberately ignore the lack of official permission to pindah. They counted on government simply accepting an established fact. This was the test case the other longhouses were awaiting without having told me. If Lubok Subong succeeded it would undermine all hope for implementing my proposals. I waited. The response came sooner than expected. The entire Lubok Subong community was returned at government's expense, having lost the bulk of their property. Individuals trickled back up the Lemanak. The haughty leader of the move dared not return and died, broken and humiliated, shortly afterwards in Simanggang. They had done, with brio, what the Iban had been doing for centuries and they had my sympathy. But their failure made our plans possible.

Not overnight, of course. But perhaps this could be the moment to negotiate a site for our centre. We have no land was the recurrent response. But I had noticed an overgrown plot beside the river and after being told this was not a graveyard decided to explore who claimed the land rights and whether it might be available. 'No' became 'perhaps' and finally 'yes' as it emerged that the area was taboo for Iban rice cultivation, as well as being haunted. This had been where, it was eventually revealed, a leper, ostracised from his longhouse, had lived and died generations ago. It would be for us to turn round the ill-omen.

The centre was wanted as an area for a school and other buildings, where I could live and those working with me. It was also needed for vegetable and fruit gardens for our use, for demonstration purposes and to provide planting material as well as for fishponds to teach fishpond culture, to produce fish for consumption and fry for distribution. The budget provided posts, on the lowest employment scale, for half a dozen local recruits. The minimum requirement was primary schooling. No Lemanak Iban qualified. The school in Simanggang, with the headmaster's glowing recommendation, presented a better educated candidate who particularly wanted to 'help his people in the interior'. He arrived and after two nights in the longhouse wrote me a long letter, in English, explaining that 'these people were too backward to help' and announced his immediate departure. He and the schoolmaster had convinced each other that it was a life-threatening place to be. Another candidate withdrew his application.

I turned to the Undup. Senior schoolchildren that I had known were interested and their families reluctantly agreed. I arranged some basic training in agricultural extension with an emphasis on vegetable gardening, fruit cultivation and fishponds, an introductory course in health and midwifery, as well as workshop experience of carpentry and outboard engine maintenance. My hope was that after six months or so I could assemble a small team of motivated young people sufficient to develop the centre and able to demonstrate skills before touring the longhouses where new practices were to be propagated. By then I was hopeful that the Lemanak Iban could be induced to jettison dreams of pindah and commit themselves to creating new life for the Lemanak.

Of course, it took a little longer and it was often tough going. But gradually, with some longhouses responding more readily than others and occasional back-pedalling, we made a beginning. By the end of the first year my 'mid-tour' leave, two weeks around the middle of the original three-year contract, was approved. The establishment officer in Kuching confirmed arrangements, I had to make my own bookings. He said, yes, many people opted to board one of the liners on the last leg of its far eastern voyage, three days from Singapore to Hong Kong and after a couple of days in Hong Kong back to Singapore. It made the perfect break, which, with a smile, he thought I fully deserved. Were any documents required: such as a visa for Hong Kong? I asked. 'No', he said, ' with a British passport you don't need a visa.' 'But I don't have a British passport.' He flushed, as head of personnel he had authorised my recruitment into the administrative service. 'You don't!' he said. 'We always knew you had a Danish background from your name, but you were so English, your education, the way you spoke, that we just assumed you had become British.' He paused. 'Why don't you become British? Doesn't it make sense?'

After my return from leave, in 1962, I submitted the relevant papers with the warm support of friends. I had been resident in Sarawak little more than two years but had lived for a very long time in England and I was duly naturalised British; I solemnly swore an oath of allegiance to Queen Elizabeth and her heirs. My Britishness was formally endorsed and a passport would be issued as soon as the consular authorities completed processing of the documentation. Meanwhile the notion of Malaysia was gathering support. The full independence of Singapore had triggered concerns for its viability and security as an independent state; close association if not integration with Malaya seemed the answer, providing Malaya direct access to the great port and Singapore with a substantial hinterland. The problem was demography.

Singapore was predominantly Chinese and Malaya already had as many Chinese in its population as the Malay leadership considered palatable. Someone had the brilliant idea of granting ultra-speedy independence to Sarawak and British North Borneo – Britain was becoming anxious to dispose of remaining colonies – and make them part of the new federation to balance the demographics on the mistaken assumption that their people were essentially Malay. Ethnically proto-Malay they might have been but they were far from identical to the Islamic Malays of the peninsula; the indigenous tribes, who constituted the majority in both colonies, practised either their traditional religion or Christianity of one brand or another and did not identify with the Islamic Malay minority amongst them. They had to be offered a range of constitutional guarantees regarding religion as well as the use of English, the language of the educated.

Prior to approval of plans for the Malaysian federation a conference in 1964 in London brought together the leaders of Malaya and Singapore. At the conference Lee Kuan Yew raised a subsidiary issue. He was nervous that many of his wealthiest Chinese entrpreneurs might prefer to maintain access to wider horizons by retaining British citizenship. He insisted on an additional and unusual clause that anyone who was British by virtue of birth, residence or naturalisation in any of the territories concerned would automatically become Malaysian. I received from the British Consulate a kind letter recognizing that, quite obviously, this condition was not intended to apply in a case such as mine but they had no authority to grant an exception. If and when I returned to reside in England they were confident my situation could be regularised. Meanwhile my next passport would be not British but Malaysian. My identity had taken an unforeseen direction.

In the Lemanak passports seemed irrelevant. The second year had not been easy but saw real progress in many areas. Fishponds and fish culture were a huge success and one of the young Undup staff communicated his remarkable flair. The rivers had been overfished and fishpond culture met the Iban appetite for fish. Vegetable gardening also prospered and fruit cultivation, including the unfamiliar but healthy papaya – once the Iban could be persuaded that it did not 'smell'.

A cholera outbreak in the Kuching area provided an unexpected boost for efforts to teach hygiene and boil river water before drinking. Medication for round worm infestation was impressively effective though pit latrines, a partial condition for medication, never became popular. First aid instruction proved surprisingly appealing. The school went from strength to strength with demands for a second school from several longhouses; adult literacy classes were also conducted. Despite experiments with wet rice planting hill rice remained the staple and with harvests continuing to fail in yielding sufficiently cash was essential to purchase rice. Rubber was being planted but took time to yield and there was a further problem when the return on small-holdings proved insufficient if the price of natural rubber on world markets declined. Block planting permitted important economies of scale and the possibility of processing rubber sheet for a higher price. But every enquiry as to where we could plant on a wider scale met the same response: no land.

Land rights were part of the problem. The Iban acquired the right to a parcel of land by felling and clearing primary forest and this was inherited by the generations following. A patchwork of parcels was one consequence. The land might become leached, useless for farming, but the Iban still remembered and watched over every square metre that they owned. They rejected amalgamation or exchange. Prospects even for a modest rubber estate seemed non-existent until I learned about the red soil. Looking optimistically toward the future I had begun exploring where a road might be built to open inaccessible land for cultivation as well as providing a useful communications link.

Between the Lemanak and the Ulu Ai stretched forest barely exploited since it lacked the rivers essential to Iban life. And much of the area was suspect in Iban eyes because the soil was reddish, supposedly blood-stained following the passage from a head-hunting expedition of a mythical hero. Soil was known to be poor throughout most of the region; reddish soil, derived from basic igneous rock, might be an exception. I begged for a soil survey to prove it. But the Iban still remained suspicious and it was only after seemingly endless nights of longhouse debate that I succeeded in gaining their confidence to proceed and was eventually able to achieve a viable rubber estate with land registered in their name. When before leaving I witnessed terraces being mapped out over an ever-widening acreage I knew that after those three years, 1961, 1962 and 1963, the Lemanak Iban, their children and grandchildren had a future in the Lemanak.

During the third year many in the longhouse-villages had come to accept that change was inevitable and that it could be in their own long-term interest. Central government, which had originally considered the project a lost cause, without telling me, and approved it only because it cost so little (I could hardly believe my eyes when years later I saw a UN budget for something vaguely comparable), started taking interest. One useful function of the scheme was to entertain international advisers, always a pain to the colonial administration. It took two days to reach us, overland and up-river by longboat, and two to return. The visiting expert was thus conveniently occupied for at least a week and could be expected to depart by the earliest available flight out, exhausted from hazardous travel, exposure to the sun, too much unfamiliar food for a delicate digestion and having slept badly. Less convenient for me.

Visitors, when they came, tended to arrive unannounced. Messages hand carried up-river were the only means of communication; I had neither telephone nor radio. Late one afternoon a longboat disgorged a small party that revolved round a partially blind Welshman. He had been successful in Nigeria, he told us and distributed illustrated pamphlets to prove it, in teaching blind farmers. His mission was to do the same in Sarawak; he would be spending one night in the Lemanak.

With dusk falling it was impossible to alert even nearby longhouses and assemble an audience, as I was requested to do. If indeed any of the Iban had wanted to listen. In one more distant longhouse there lived a blind man but he was well integrated in the life of his family. The only other partially sighted man known to us was a manang medicine man, whose handicap was a professional qualification. That our visitor, this individual, with support staff, had been dispatched, without advance warning, all the way from Kuching was absurd. I can only imagine that it arose from a well-intentioned Commonwealth project and the inability of those responsible to see how it might be applied in Sarawak: well – send him up to the Lemanak scheme.

Bobanau was a committed man; he was not to be fobbed off by insufficient blind people. He insisted on delivering his message. That evening I assembled the staff and anyone passing by. Bobanau took himself very seriously and he described in great detail the value of compost to gardening of almost any variety, as he had demonstrated in Nigeria. This rudimentary element was easy to produce, required neither special skills nor expensive additives. He explained how to pile up vegetable waste and to add urine and to turn the mass. Urine, he repeated, was invaluable to compost-making and it was easy enough for the men to contribute. For a moment I feared he was about to clarify the objection to women's urine. Compost he repeated so often in closing his lecture that it became his signature. He departed down-river the following day with no blind encounters to report but was long remembered as Mr Kompos.

On another occasion an Englishman disembarked unexpectedly. He introduced himself as Dr George Wadsworth, regional nutrition adviser from World Health Organisation. A charming man, interested in all we were doing, who never once complained about the simple food on our table. I was no nutritionist. My feeding policy and practice were based on a basic formula: some stodge, which in that context could only mean rice; veg, home grown, and a little protein, usually salt fish or paste, cheap, widely available and long-lasting even in equatorial heat and humidity. Modest variety from the vegetables we grew, different types of salt fish and sometimes tinned sardine, fish from our fish-ponds when available, our own eggs, and very, very occasionally game helped enliven the menu. Dr Wadsworth approved the diet. He also approved the way we applied this as a model in seeking to improve nutrition in the longhouses, which he visited. We enjoyed having a visitor who was unfailingly polite to the Iban and to us all. I was sorry to see him leave but pleased with his very positive assessment of what we were trying to achieve and how we went about it. I received no official report and heard nothing further, not that I expected to.

9 Invitation and the wider world

Months later arrived hand-delivered a large envelope sent from WHO regional headquarters in Manila. It contained an invitation to participate in a 1964 conference on how to improve nutritional standards at the village level. Travel expenses would be paid and a small *per diem*, and it was suggested that I visit at least one project comparable to my own in TPNG, the Territory of Papua and New Guinea, or perhaps New Caledonia en route to the Philippines. Was the Sarawak Government going to agree? Sarawak, though becoming independent as a state of Malaysia, had yet to begin making itself independent of British colonial administrative procedure.

The initial response was dubious. Eventually, on two stringent conditions, one, that there would be no cost whatsoever to the Sarawak government, and, two, that every day of absence would be charged to my accrued leave entitlement, I was authorised to go. After three years in the Lemanak and having achieved a degree of success that no one had expected I bade our team a tearful farewell and prepared to leave the unrecognisably more friendly and forward-looking Iban with whom I had struggled. WHO provided a travel reward: flights via Sydney to reach TPNG then administered by Australia, onwards to the Philippines and return.

Australian culture shock began when the taxi driver called me 'mate' and had me sit next to him. That was nothing compared to the culture shock of New Guinea. Borneo was sophisticated by Papuan standards. To direct the occasional car at what seemed the only crossroads in Port Moresby stood a policeman: digger hatted, crisply uniformed, but without shoes, and because shoeless standing on a doormat. The local patois, purportedly English in origin, was partially intelligible: 'bugger up' meant to go wrong and was in frequent use. That pencil was *'bleistift'* reminded visitors that the territory had once been German. Other vocabulary, drawn from the most basic Australian usage, albeit crude was all too easy to understand. Away from the capital indigenous women walked piglets on a lead and, yes, I saw it, suckled them. The men wore flamboyant decorations projecting through their nostrils and little else.

The mountainous interior was dramatically beautiful. Suddenly it was all around me as the pilot banked the two-seater aircraft to drop us through a thick mass of cloud and deposit me in a lush valley. The engine still turning the pilot raised a thumb, swivelled the plane about for take-off and disappeared back into the clouds. In New Guinea a pilot was either a good pilot or a dead pilot, they told me before take-off; most were ex World War II, many from the Luftwaffe. They also told me that the local project manager would send transport as soon as he heard an aircraft land.

Stranded in the field I surveyed a landscape as if somewhere in Switzerland or Austria, untouched, without a human presence. Nothing could have been more peaceful. All was still. That was when three spear-carrying, nose-enhanced, Afro-haired men emerged from nowhere. I smiled. They stared. I smiled again. I tried speaking a south-east Asian dialect, and another. They grunted. One man made a noise at the others. All three shuffled, regrasped their spears. Then they turned from me and were gone. I would have walked had I known which way to go. I was beginning to wonder whether my landing had escaped notice when a land cruiser came bumping overland.

The project manager, an American missionary, could not have been kinder. The project, unfortunately, bore not the slightest resemblance to mine; the missionary and his young family lived a clean-cut *Saturday Evening Post* life in a well-appointed modern bungalow in the heart of New Guinea with American food, drink and other essentials flown in; he was trying to learn a local language, he told me, but there were so many.

On my return to Mount Hagen I was to meet the divisional medical and health officer. I expected another Australian, like most official expatriates in TPNG, rough and ready Australians, who dressed and spoke accordingly. Instead a fine-featured man, wearing well-pressed trousers, a silk shirt and ascot, came to greet me. His accent was anything but Australian as he introduced himself by a middle European name. Had I been a woman he would surely have kissed my hand. All very perplexing and I wondered what Somerset Maugham material had abandoned this refined man in mid-New Guinea. In Port Moresby I heard. He had been a professor of gynaecology in Budapest, successful and internationally respected. After the Hungarian uprising he escaped. He was offered asylum in Australia but the Australian Medical Association refused to recognise his professional qualifications, distinguished surgeon though he was. He faced labouring on the railroad or washing dishes. An alternative ordeal was a five year assignment in TPNG after which he would be authorised to practice medicine in Australia. I hope he succeeded. He proved delightful and unexpected company that evening.

New Caledonia had been dropped from my itinerary. Not by me, but by the authorising authority in Manila, presumably. So I flew to the Philippines. If I expected them to be much like Malaysia I was mistaken. A very different society projected itself: conspicuous wealth, Cadillacs with blacked out windows, gated mansions, flamboyant dress, paraded beside equally conspicuous poverty and a galaxy of girlie bars. As George Wadsworth said on driving into town: 'Where you have poverty you find cheap female labour.'

Manila was lively and I enjoyed the conference. To my surprise I was the only 'expert' who had personally planned, applied and lived through the process of improving nutritional standards at the village level. The recipe was straightforward, easy to describe and illustrate, leaving ample post-conference energy. Over drinks I chatted to a young Frenchwoman. She smoked, as most did in those days, and I usually carried matches. My last match spluttered and she fumbled for a lighter in her handbag. That was when I saw the pistol. An elegant ivory handled pistol. She saw that I saw. 'You carry a gun?' I said. 'Oh yes,' she said, 'in the Philippines you have to, everyone does.' Another big difference with Malaysia where gun control was strictly enforced.

I carried no gun the penultimate evening when a congenial group celebrated the meeting's success. We had moved from one bar to a second when midnight approached. Time to go home. I was offered a lift but preferred walking in the fresh night air. We were on the bay and I knew how to reach the Bayview Hotel, or so I thought. As I walked the distance seemed to increase. There were fewer and fewer street lamps. It became sense to take a taxi. We visitors had been scrupulously instructed to be wary of taxis. Golden cabs and Yellow cabs were reliable; only they could be trusted.

Few cabs passed: none were Golden or Yellow. Despairing I decided to hail whatever came. 'Bayview Hotel' I told the driver very distinctly. He nodded and repeated 'Bayview.' The hotel was well-known, further down the esplanade. I sat back only to jerk upright when the taxi took a right hand turning. 'Bayview Hotel' I said again, firmly; he nodded, mumbling 'Bayview.' I assumed he had to approach the hotel from the side. Only when we crossed a long viaduct was it blatantly obvious that we were off course. 'Bayview Hotel' I repeated yet again, more assertively. 'Yes, Bayview,' he said vaguely, driving on.

By then, of course, I knew we were heading away from the hotel. We had left the centre of town. We drove through grubby streets with little illumination. In the distance I spotted a service station, lit, and ordered the driver to pull in. He went straight past. I wasn't sure whether to rabbit punch him, thus certainly crashing the car, and I had no experience of rabbit punching anyone except a rabbit. That was when I opened both back doors. He would be sure to stop. He drove on regardless, doors flapping. It became rather cold. After some minutes I closed the doors again.

I had just closed the doors when the taxi swerved right down a side street, stopping in front of a non-descript house. I got out, repeated 'Bayview Hotel' to the driver as severely as I could and walked purposefully on. He called after me. Then shouted 'You pay fare.' I stopped, turned, and with all the authority I could muster said: 'I pay fare when we reach Bayview Hotel.' The moment I continued walking someone whistled. Suddenly two burly individuals emerged from the surrounding gloom, one on my left, the other to my right. For the first time in my life I prepared to use force, real force. As the left side man grabbed me by the elbow I clenched the fist of my free arm and thumped him in the stomach as hard as I could, the only time I had hit to hurt. He loosened his grip. At the same time I dug my right elbow aggressively into the other fellow. And ran. 'You come back, you pay fare,' echoed plaintively as I ran as fast as I possibly could towards a better-lit road a couple of hundred yards away. I heard steps, in pursuit, then they faltered, and the car did not follow, and no one fired.

When I finally reached the better-lit road a Yellow cab just happened to be passing. I had not the breath to call but the driver noticed me waving. He asked no questions and delivered me promptly to the Bayview Hotel. Next day I was told that I had been exceptionally fortunate not to be knifed or shot at.

Fire-arms and joy-riding apart Manila introduced me to a new world, the world of international organisation. At WHO regional headquarters, as well as those with medical qualifications, I met a UNESCO community development officer, whose work was quite similar to mine, and a Swiss interpreter about to join UNDP (United Nations Development Programme). Jean-Pierre Schellenberg, the Swiss, wondered whether I had ever contemplated being employed by the UN. I would qualify, he thought, given my academic background and practical experience. The United Nations, as concept and ideal, had long attracted me. I knew next to nothing about working there and had previously encountered no one who did.

My project in the Lemanak was at an end. Sarawak had become independent in 1963. The white man era was rapidly winding down. I had no desire to leave Sarawak and the Iban though sensed it might be time to depart. The Sarawak government asked me to stay. War with Indonesia, Konfrontasi, arising from Soekarno's crazed assertion that Malaysia was an imperial plot to encircle Indonesia, intensified through an unlikely alliance with a clandestine communist movement. Armed incursions across the border, into places where I had been living, and the constant threat of attack disrupted Iban life. The first military commander tasked with our defence wanted all Iban evacuated from a five-mile belt so as to be free to shoot whatever moved. That made no sense in the jungle, which gave cover to invaders while his troops shot only orang-utan. And in so vast an area the mainly British Ghurka regiments deployed would never muster sufficient manpower to cope with infiltration.

The next CO understood. Instead of evacuating the Iban, bring them on side. Their information would contribute to monitoring alien activity. It would be for us to win their hearts and minds, and ensure their willingness to share information. A people traditionally well-disposed towards their rulers was being subverted. Anti-Malaysia elements, communist as well as Indonesian, sought to convince the Iban that fighting was a consequence of Malaysia, that Indonesian forces fought only to restore Sarawak to itself. Competition for Iban hearts and minds became intense and I was wanted to help.

Because I spoke Iban and was known by reputation in much of the area, I was to visit longhouses along the border and explain what Malaysia was intended to achieve and describe the acquisitive threat from Indonesia. A raid in which Indonesian soldiers invaded a longhouse and appropriated rice bolstered my argument. The Iban response to my visits was encouraging. A key isolated longhouse close to the frontier was difficult to reach and dangerous, according to the military, and accessible only if further helicopter hours could be spared. At short notice a chopper became available.

The Royal Navy pilot invited me up front to the co-pilot's seat – there were never enough flying hours for co-pilotage. Orders were to fly below tree level following twisting rivers which was almost more dangerous than enemy fire, or go high out of range of enemy small arms. We ascended to a superb view over dense forest and the Kapuas lakes before dropping to an improvised landing-site. I delivered my message, answered varied questions, provided what reassurance I could and off we flew back up above the canopy. Wonderfully peaceful the vast landscape appeared. Until I heard the pilot desperately trying to make radio contact. He pointed ahead. A distant fighter aircraft was heading for us. 'Tulip calling buttercup' the pilot repeated and repeated and repeated. No response. A week before an officer seated beside the pilot had been killed. I remember vividly what went through my mind: if they shoot me, so be it, but if they shoot the pilot how would I possibly operate the controls before me to fly the chopper. That was the moment tulip reached buttercup. The fighter was not Indonesian but an RAF jet providing cover for a plodding Hastings making a wide circuit to drop supplies at a military border-post.

The hearts and minds campaign had advantages. Funds, previously in drastically short supply, became available for rural development. We were able to build simple bridges and minor roads. My modest project had scored wider resonance and I was invited to become responsible for development across a large region. That I could not refuse and two exciting years passed all too quickly.

Malaysia and the war with Indonesia enveloped our world and introduced new faces. Not only the military, Nepalese as well as British, Sarawak and Malaysian Rangers, but volunteers notably the Peace Corps and other internationals. Children at our local Engkilili bazaar stared open-mouthed at the first black man they had seen when an African-American arrived with the peace corps while a white American volunteer confused everyone by insisting he was not 'European', the official translation for 'orang puteh' which meant literally 'white man'.

Less amusing was the threat posed by the clandestine communist organization. In the Lemanak a Chinese worker was reported as visiting longhouses where he sang communist propaganda songs, though the impact was muted since he sang in Chinese, which the Iban did not understand. Some months later he was shot while guiding Indonesian invaders on a border raid. I heard the news when I happened to pass through an unwontedly tense and silent Engkilili, but the tension had another source. No one would explain. From a friend in the bazaar I eventually gouged the reason.

Bong Nam Song had been arrested. Bong was a leading shop-keeper, among the earliest in Engkilili where he had always lived; he was known for his good relations with the Iban whose language he spoke well. What was the charge? I asked. Nobody knew. He had been abruptly arrested without charge, and immediately escorted away. Still no charge when days later I enquired again. I reacted with my most impetuous decision ever. We were fighting, as far as I was concerned, not for territory but for principle, for a free society governed by law.

I had business in Kuching and made that reason to travel to the capital and ask for an appointment with the State Secretary. He knew me – just – having been briefed on my achievement in the Lemanak, but my effrontery still shocks me. I was a junior official and Tony Shaw headed the state government at a difficult time. He agreed to see me. Once in his office I delivered the statement that I had been turning over and over in my mind. I had been proud, I said, of serving the Sarawak government and was committed to the principles for which we fought, including the rule of law. I was resigning. I could not remain in a service that condoned arbitrary arrest without charge. (On the journey to Kuching as I reflected on the implications of resignation I had come to recognise the enormous courage of those Germans who openly opposed the Nazi regime despite wives and families and mortgages and professional careers. I was not married and youthfully confident that I could find other employment.) Shaw heard me out. 'Go and sit over there,' he said after a moment, pointing to a conference desk, 'and read the documents I am sending for.'

A bundle of papers, marked 'top secret' was brought him; he nodded, and the documents were placed before me. The original papers were in Chinese but all had been meticulously translated. They made frightening reading: the large scale purchase of explosives, acquisition of arms, weapons training and plans for attack on administrative and police posts to be coordinated by clandestine communist organization infiltrators, and suggestions that where possible action in Sarawak be harmonised with Indonesian political involvement and military incursion. Names appeared intermittently; I noticed Bong more than once.

Shaw gave me an hour to digest the file then 'Well, what do you think?' This was treason, plotting to overthrow the state by armed force, there was no denying, it was all too apparent. 'Why not charge him?' The evidence was there. 'We want to trace one or two of his collaborators before it all gets into the press. I give you my word that within two weeks he will be charged.' I took note appreciatively, thanked the State Secretary warmly for his great courtesy in giving me so much of his time and confidential attention. As I was leaving he smiled, saying: 'So you won't be resigning, will you.'

The old ways were affected also by other intrusions. The Peace Corps was coming to Sarawak and I was chosen to brief them during training but their code discouraged social interaction with British expatriates, labelled imperialists – quite unlike the benevolent Americans as in Vietnam; Anthony Burgess' *Time for a Tiger* was prescribed reading. In Kuching on other business I met Derrick Reddish, who had long experience in Sarawak, to discuss problems facing up-river communities, and when the meeting ended, he asked whether I would like to accompany him and a friend next day on an excursion to the coast; he had a speedboat at his disposal.

That was when I asked June, who had been in Simanggang aspiring to a Peace Corps assignment in the Lemanak before being reassigned. Rather than spend most of the day pretending not to be there she declined. Derrick had called in the morning, apologising profusely, to say he could not come but that was no reason to cancel. The speedboat would be available as planned. I was bathing from the muddy beach when a raucous party of young Chinese arrived. They vanished for an elaborate picnic lunch and it was late afternoon before they reappeared. Ominous clouds and choppy water foretold a storm. My speedboat driver rejected any thought of setting off and we were startled to see the Chinese embarking in an obviously overloaded longboat. They were still in sight when the storm broke. Great waves crashed everywhere. I watched as the longboat overturned and its passengers were disgorged into the unfriendly sea. Some clutched at the overturned hull, some swam ineptly towards the shore, the rest screamed and splashed throwing their arms about in an attempt to remain afloat. The speedboat driver had swiftly moved to rescue as many as he could. A few of the Chinese managed with difficulty to approach the shore but one or two, who could not really swim, began to panic.

I had waded into the water when I became aware of a young woman screaming as the waves submerged her. She was twenty to thirty yards out. I am not a fast swimmer and had no life-saving experience but I am confident in water and struggled to her just as she was going under again and helped her use me as a buoy. She raised herself enough to lift her head and swallow two huge gulps of air. Not quick but strong enough as a swimmer to support her weight I brought her to the beach, undrowned.

That was when I noticed another Chinese shouting for help, arms and legs thrashing about in a frantic attempt to stay afloat. I went back out but the young man, it was a man, had lost all self-control and instead of using me for support began climbing over me, pushing me under. For a few strokes I continued trying to swim but was reaching the end of my tether when, as he pushed me heavily under again, my foot touched bottom. We both made it ashore. Only afterwards did I learn that one of the Chinese party had been drowned, leading to an inquest. After the proceedings I was profusely thanked by the Chinese woman whose life, as she insisted, I had saved. And I received from the Chief Secretary a letter paying tribute to my disregard for personal safety in saving the young Chinese. Unofficially, I was told that an award would have been recommended had there been an independent witness.

Before my contract ended by 1966 the government offered me a further appointment with still greater responsibility. But much as I loved Sarawak, I knew instinctively that an expatriate would not long be accepted in a position of authority, visible as well as powerful. In a technical or professional capacity, medical, agricultural, engineering, there was less of a problem, but not high profile administration. My ally, the State Secretary, endeavoured to persuade me: Sarawak was not like that, he insisted. A year later both he and the State Financial Secretary were obliged to depart before completing their terms of office. Better, I thought, to have left while still wanted.

The long sea journey back to Europe gave ample time to regret leaving. I missed the people, their warmth and the amber tone of their skin, I missed the country, the colour of it and the sunlight if rather less the equatorial rainfall, and I missed my work. But one advantage of old school colonial service was the lengthy leave that followed every three unbroken years serving abroad. I would devote that to preparing anthropological papers based on my Iban experience. It was one way to retain the bond. I was busy putting preliminary order in my notes one morning when a fellow passenger apologised for interrupting, and could he ask me a question. For three weeks on an ocean liner, with little to do except play bridge it is not uncommon to pass the time being inquisitive. I nodded politely. 'It's true, Mr Jensen, isn't it,' the accent was American, 'that you have a degree from Harvard, and from Oxford. And you have been working for years somewhere in the Borneo interior. Gees, Mr Jensen, what happened?'

10 Travels towards the UN

AFTER NAVIGATING THE SUEZ CANAL our first port of call was Naples with an excursion organised to Pompeii. Anyone suggesting a few years earlier that I should feel at home in Italy would have been joking. But now I felt European, that my roots were in Europe, this was where I belonged and with all the Latin and Greek absorbed at school Italy and Pompeii were parts of my world. As England continued to be. Back in London I saw George Wadsworth, pleasant as ever. Though an academic career appealed, and I had revived my Oxford links, I did not abandon thoughts of the UN. After Manila J-P Schellenberg had sent me the details of a UNESCO community development post in Vietnam, or Cambodia, I forget, only to follow this with a letter saying the position had been filled.

Wadsworth insisted his contacts were all medical but he did know one person in New York, who might be helpful, Julia Henderson; I could try writing to her. I did. First problem: was she Mrs or Miss? Wadsworth had no idea. That was a time when many women took this seriously, and Ms meant a manuscript. I solved the difficulty by addressing her as Dr. She had no doctorate, she was to tell me later, instead assuming I had one, but the letter was correctly forwarded to Personnel. I received an uninspiring acknowledgement and a form to complete. This was done. I waited. And waited.

Uncertain how my application to the UN would fare, I applied for and was a awarded a modest six-month research grant. Lacking experience of international organisations I wrote politely to inform Personnel that I would not be available for the next six months. In response I received a clumsily worded letter advising me that the UN could not foresee requirements that far ahead but to apply again when I became available.

'To hell with you' I remember thinking and reverted to anthropology. Just days later, as unexpected as it was to my delight, I received an invitation to lecture on Sarawak and the Iban at a Peace Corps training programme in Hawaii. Before travelling to Hawaii the research project was to take me briefly to Cairo, Delhi and Bangkok, with a stopover in Sarawak permitted for personal reasons. Two incidents in Delhi made that visit memorable. My hotel, the relic of another era, had a vast echoing dining hall, vintage ceiling fans, labouring to stir the air, made the only sound. Diners were few and quietly spoken. An impressive, grandly uniformed and turbaned Sikh served me a plate with curry and a chapatti . When he next approached my table I asked whether I might have some rice. He raised himself to his full height and boomed: 'Don't you know there is famine in India!' The other diners duly stared at me as if I alone did not know that rice was served only every other day and chapatti every other day. The other incident leaves a pleasanter memory. I took a couple of hours off to visit old Delhi and do some drawing and was standing with my pen poised when someone nudged me. A young man had been dispatched by the store-keeper to bring me a stool. I smiled by way of thank you and sat down. Minutes later my drawing began flapping; the young man had been assigned as my punkah-wallah. The drawing was speckled with haphazard black spots, some of which could be integrated into buildings and merchandise with those overhead being converted into crows.

The programmed two weeks in Hawaii with prospective Peace Corpsmen and women were extended to two very agreeable months. The Course Director, Jake Stalker, was an energetic character, about to remarry, again, this time to a long-haired blonde, who liked his dry martinis. He was less conventional in other respects and it was his imaginative approach to administration that extended my stay. We discussed it over drinks before lunch. I was still too colonial for dry martinis and ordered gin and bitter lemon, London's long drink of the time. The American-speaking bartender repeated 'gin and bit'o lemon' twice before giving me neat gin with a small lemon segment and was confused when I then wanted tonic.

Stalker, meanwhile, had already been on the phone. My extension was approved even before I could agree. No triple copies, signed and counter-signed, memos ascending a hierarchical chain of command for ultimate approval. That appealed. And I was tempted when Stalker started explaining about the East-West Center where there might be an opening for me. My Oxford research degree was relevant but I needed a 'Phud'. With a PhD in view I returned to England two months later. Before departing Hawaii one of my fellow 'resource persons' with whom I had become friendly insisted that I join him and his visiting parents for dinner. The mother said how much she had heard about me and what a good friend I was of her son, it was a real pleasure meeting me. Over coffee she wanted to hear more about my plans. When I mentioned interest in the UN she became enthusiastic: then I would be coming to America and could become a citizen, her finest accolade, but not my ambition.

On the return journey to England I stopped over in New York. An old friend from Harvard days had me revisit some familiar places, first checking that I had seen the Empire State building, the Chrysler building, Grand Central, the Plaza, et cetera. When I admitted to never having seen the UN, he insisted. Over lunch in a diner on Second Avenue I mentioned the correspondence with Personnel. John, my friend, urged me to phone. He even gave me a coin when I did not have the right change. In that more human era a telephonist answered. I asked for Personnel. Who? she asked. I vaguely remembered a signature from the first letter, Slater. 'We have no one of that name' said the telephonist, 'but could it be Salter?' Yes, I thought it could be, and she put me through. As luck would have it – and knowing the UN as I came to, this was really lucky – Miss Salter took the phone. I referred to the exchange of letters, said I happened to be in New York. She asked a question or two before suggesting that I come in the following Tuesday. I would be gone by then. Monday, she proposed. It was Thursday and I was leaving at the weekend. Then she said: 'Tomorrow, Friday, in the early afternoon.' I thanked her.

Before departing New York I had been interviewed by Julia Henderson, when having glanced at my file she said she did not have a doctorate, and others, and given more forms to complete. An offer of appointment seemed imminent: in the Secretariat, in the Department of Economic and Social Affairs. I naively assumed that, like the only service I knew, headquarters assignments rotated with field postings, and that UNDP was the field arm where I saw my future. In the months following I recalled that inability to foresee requirements six months ahead. Recruitment took only marginally less, which afforded me time to complete library research for my doctoral dissertation and much of an initial draft. Finally, in April 1967 I sailed for New York to take up a probationary appointment as P3 step1.

P3 step1 meant nothing to me when I accepted. Personnel assessed it from my age, 33, and salary level in Sarawak. Sarawak salaries bore no relevance to income levels or the cost of living in New York. I became fond of recounting that, as a personal experiment when first in Borneo, I lived for half a year on the equivalent of 100 US dollars a month. Not an experiment to be repeated in New York. But the salary concerned me little – I grew up with austerity during and just after the war, was educated at an English boarding school, had spent nearly seven years in primitive Sarawak conditions, and was a bachelor – what mattered was the level of responsibility. From having had some influence on major investment, even where roads should be built and bridges sited, dealing directly with politicians and top administrators, submitting official reports and working all hours, I found I was not authorised to sign many of the letters that I drafted. People went home at five or five-thirty at latest; passers-by seeing lights on late into the evening imagined the UN still working but it was the cleaners. Office closed on Saturdays. This was a world so different from that I had known. And a far cry from the idealistic commitment I associated with the UN, of being personally engaged in work of global importance. Though every morning when I walked down forty-second street from the Tudor Hotel, which had to be pronounced 'two-door' for any American to understand, where breakfast cost ninety-nine cents to scrape under the taxable rate, and entered the court, long before cumbersome security apparatus blocked access, the soaring building and massed flags elated me. I loved the fountains playing round Barbara Hepworth's beautiful 'Single form', which resembled, on a massively greater scale, a piece of driftwood I had shaped in Sarawak. The sculpture had been donated, the plaque said, at the wish of Dag Hammarskjöld. And Hammarskjold, I knew, worked round the clock.

Julia Henderson, my division director, was also a worker, it transpired. Her energy was famous. 'Doesn't she get tired?' people asked when she travelled; 'No, never,' said her assistant, 'but we do!' The UN promoted the ambitious capital projects that were the fashion, industrialisation, major transport infrastructure, gigantic dams for energy, vast commercial agriculture like the African ground-nut scheme. Confident economic projections abounded, theory nourished by optimism. No one was much interested in my modest development experience. Tiny scale projects seemed largely irrelevant. Schumacher had yet to make small beautiful. To me it remained self-evident that to be accepted, endure and prosper projects in developing countries had to have roots in that society, relate to its values and be manageable. I knew something else that no one took seriously at the time: Islam would be a force in the world.

Having lived in a partly Muslim state and close to great Muslim lands I foresaw Islam's political dimension. Under-developed countries were renamed 'developing' by way of encouragement, then third world. The genius of Raul Prebisch realised that this utterly disparate grouping, with little or nothing in common except relative poverty, had voting power if voting as a bloc. He invented the Group of 77. The inaugural United Nations Conference on Trade and Development proved his point. It gave the developing world leverage in

UN councils. It did not confer pride. Prebisch, as a Christian Argentinian, was unlikely to have considered Islam. Whereas sailing back from south-east Asia, from Malaysia, by way of Indonesia, skirting the Bay of Bengal with Bangladesh in the distance, to Pakistan, round Aden and the Persian Gulf, through the Suez canal and Egypt, and along the north African coast past Libya, Tunisia, Algeria and Morocco brought vividly home to me how huge a swathe of the world was Islamic. Islam spanned the globe across Asia, the middle east and much of Africa. It brought together countries otherwise quite unalike and distinguished them from Christendom, Europe and European civilisation implanted in America, north and south, and Australasia, and it gave them pride. Admittedly, I did not foresee OPEC, the extraordinary rise in the price of oil, and the avalanche of wealth it showered on the navel of Islam. That, of course, provided the resources, power. Given all that has happened in recent years I suspect that, even without those means, the Muslim world would have insisted on having its importance duly recognised, on having a voice. In New York in the late sixties I found no one to take me seriously. I only wish I had published my thoughts, if I could have found a publisher. War in the middle east provided a more media obsessive focus.

If not the worst of times, times were bad. To universal surprise, the Israelis, instead of being driven into the sea, defeated Egypt leaving the Arabs humiliated. The Jews were cock-a-hoop, defended by the American veto, but insecure. The UN stood by, marginalised it looked to a junior member of the secretariat perched in the visitors' gallery, and impressed with Abba Eban's extraordinary eloquence showing the Security Council apparently impervious to argument. Prague had its spring and relapsed into harder communism. Biafra seceded from Nigeria and Nigeria went to unforgiving war to restore the federation. In April 1968 Martin Luther King, Jr was assassinated and two months later they murdered Bobbie Kennedy, the president John Kennedy's idealistic younger brother. Even Manhattan was a dangerous place.

Walking home from dinner with Barbara, an American friend, we saw an elderly woman stumble and fall. Instinctively I moved to help only to have Barbara restrain me forcibly. 'But she's fallen,' I said, 'Let's help her up.' Barbara insisted it could be a trap, a set-up. 'This happens all the time,' she said, and we walked past, good Christians both. It shocked me almost as much when told always to carry bills worth fifty dollars, no more, but no less: the price of a fix. A UN colleague recounted just two days later that he had been accosted in the elevator and at knife point surrendered his wallet – containing fifty dollars. You learnt never to saunter, to stroll dreamily. You kept your eyes and wits about you and when there were few people around gave others a wide berth or crossed the road. Under overpass or bridge, over subway gratings where sooty heat wafted upwards, lived vagrants, drop-outs, misfits, rejecting or rejected by society. Supermarket trolleys barricaded their assortment of plastic bags, filthy bedding and miscellaneous rubbish. They looked resentfully, or so it seemed, sullen and silent, at every passer-by who approached their private space. I felt vaguely threatened as I had never done in the jungle or indeed in any far eastern city. Violence hung like the humidity in the air.

Students for a Democratic Society propagated revolutionary ideas. Young people from wealthy families turned against the society that privileged them, with guns and explosives. Pattie Hurst, the most famous – she made the cover of *Time* magazine – like the Weathermen had high ideals: to destroy their own prosperous world. Unexpectedly I encountered them. As a friend of another guest I had been asked to a small dinner party in a superb New York townhouse, a historic building in Greenwich village, Dustin Hoffman was a neighbour someone mentioned. Dinner was elegantly served in a dining-room furnished with antiques. In the drawing-room I identified the painter of at least one of the paintings. The host had me sit next to him while I admired his pictures and offered me brandy. He was interested, or pretended to be, in my knowledge of art and of my background, and wanted to know where in England, which he knew well, members of my family lived. I asked after his family. He had a daughter, he said, from whom, sadly, he was estranged, but she had the key to the house, and she would always be welcome home. The hostess, when I thanked her profusely for their generous hospitality, said they hoped to see me again perhaps after they returned from their holiday in the Caribbean, where they were going next day.

Two days later it was headline news. A bomb had exploded in an exclusive Manhattan townhouse. It was not immediately known how many people had been killed; a naked woman was thought to have been seen running from the burning building. Facts gradually emerged from the debris. What had at first been believed due to leaking gas had been caused by the premature explosion of a bomb being assembled by members of the Weather Underground. An ambitious bomb factory in the basement caused massive destruction and it took time to piece together the human remains. Three leaders of the Weather Underground had been killed outright, two, who were not in the basement when the dynamite exploded survived with lesser wounds. One escaped and despite being on the FBI most wanted list remained at large for a decade before surrendering herself to the authorities. She was the daughter.

Even without the Weathermen life was anything but dull for a young man in New York. Given fifty dollars in my wallet and constantly on the alert I walked and walked. I explored the city, enjoyed the electricity, the aliveness of it. I liked the endless activity on the avenues, in Central Park, down towards the village and the steel bands, competing musicians, making a great folk festival of the summer months. At that age friendships were easy to make and in the UN I discovered a lovely young woman with whom I had long conversations.

Aung San Suu Kyi was sophisticated, travelled and spoke English beautifully; we reminisced at length about the Oxford we had in common and which we both loved. It transpired that she was the daughter of Aung San, the revered hero of Burma's independence struggle who was assassinated just before the country became independent. She was intensely proud of her father, for her the ultimate role model, though I did not foresee this fine-boned, frail-looking, almost delicate young woman emulating that tough military man. Suu was ending a short contract and to my regret she left soon after. I would not see her again but followed her extraordinary career after she returned to Myanmar, as Burma had become to lead another independence movement.

Outside the UN I also made friends. A Malaysian diplomat discovered my Sarawak connection and insisted on introducing me to others with links to the region. These included a young Malay painter recently graduated from the Royal Academy Schools in London spending a year in New York on a John D. Rockefeller fellowship. Ibrahim Hussein and I talked painting and visited exhibitions together; he was endlessly creative wanting to experiment with film, engraving, screen printing and his invented 'printage' as well as novel oil painting techniques. Oil painting was his principal medium, until he fell for acrylic, and he had with him several pictures from his final show in London.

With two other friends we were in Ibrahim's apartment near the Lincoln Center when he mentioned selling. He had approached a couple of galleries and awaited the response. Rather tentatively I asked whether he would let me make an offer. He produced a painting. Though not my favourite I liked it well enough. Price? An awkward pause before Ib said he would go into the bathroom and run hot water till the mirror steamed up; with his finger he would write a figure on the misty glass. For me to decide: if acceptable fine, if not that too would be fine. The price, when I saw it before evaporation, was very fair. My means were limited but I could just afford it. I bought Ibrahim's 'Chinese actor' painting because it was a well realised early work, a vivid picture, which reminded me not only of Ib but expressed Malaysia. I did not think of it as an investment. But Ibrahim Hussein went on to be recognised as a great painter throughout his region and beyond with a museum gallery in Langkawi built exclusively to celebrate his work and commanding prices at auction far, far beyond what would fit on a bathroom mirror.

New York was not where I expected to live out my life and assignments at the UN were far from living up to expectation. When Shirley Hazzard's *Defeat of an Ideal* was published they told me she had previously worked in my division, and that was where she began writing her depressing *People in Glasshouses*. She manifestly did not suffer from any old-fashioned loyalty. I was becoming disillusioned with my ability to contribute to the ideal UN, which she desecrated and in which I still wanted to believe. To compensate I worked one full day every weekend finalising my doctoral dissertation for submission to Oxford and made plans to revert to academic life at the end of the two-year contract.

The summer of 1968 was hot and humid, as New York summers are, but the city bristled with colour and action. On the steps opposite the UN, where swords are permanently beaten into 'plowshares' and before they named the plaza in honour of Ralph Bunche, demonstrations contributed almost daily entertainment. I remember vividly one of the most colourful and the loudest. A mass of large brown bodies, flamboyantly arrayed in exuberant west African style, singing, and dancing to their own music, and waving placards for Biafra. Biafra had been the Eastern Region of Nigeria before declaring independence. The Federal government went to war to restore the federation and by the summer of 1968 Biafra had been surrounded, was effectively under siege. Biafra's supporters, in Europe as in America, campaigned energetically to enlist humanitarian and political support. Federal forces were accused of genocide. 'That's where we ought to be, doing something about that,' I said to a friend as we watched.

Heat and humidity in the city had led me to renting for August a small sub-rural apartment. A colleague was going on extended leave. We were in the same department, much the same age, and chatting one day about holiday plans when he mentioned his concern at having his place unoccupied. We did a deal. On his last Friday in the office he handed me the keys and I wished him and his family an enjoyable time home in the Netherlands. They planned to spend a week or more driving round before visiting his parents then hers.

The following Monday I was at my desk when the acting director called. Did I by any chance happen to know where Morsinck was? They needed to reach him. In fact, I did. He was touring in Holland. Did I have a contact number for him? Yes and no; I had a number where he could be found in about ten days time. 'Oh,' said the acting director. The same afternoon I was summoned. They had been trying by various means to track down Morsinck, without success. He was wanted for a mission. He was driving around with his family for a few days at the start of the holiday, he happened to have told me. Was there any way of reaching him? I thought not. The acting Director cleared his throat and assumed his most authoritative manner. Would I be willing to leave on mission, at short notice? 'Of course,' I said, before even asking when, what or where. He was not authorised to say more. I was told to stand by for a summons to be interviewed on the 38th floor.

11 Nigeria and civil war

THE 38TH FLOOR, the executive office of the Secretary-General, was close-carpeted, exclusive and impressively still. A security officer showed me to an office where I met Nils Gussing. Gussing worked for the UN High Commissioner for Refugees. He had recently completed a special if modest assignment relating to displaced persons in the middle east. Hubert Morsinck, in that area before being transferred to New York, had been made his assistant, which was the reason his name had now been mentioned. Gussing's new mission was more important but deliberately low profile.

U Thant, the Secretary-General, a profoundly humane man, was deeply concerned about the Nigerian civil war, but neither the Security Council, nor the Organisation of African Unity, nor any major power, wanted the UN politically involved. The United States and Britain both had oil interests, the Soviet Union backed federal Nigeria also with armaments, China in those days played no role, though France might be looking to benefit from opportunities arising. Even if its current President was the Frenchified Togolese Diallo Telli – he was to come through Lagos suited in dark blue with a Homburg hat, the Organisation of African Unity upheld its position of principle opposing any attempt to realign existing frontiers.

Secessionist Biafra did have supporters. It developed an effective public relations programme, through the Swiss agency Mark Press, reaching millions in Europe and north America. Federal Nigeria was accused of genocide. The predominantly Christian Ibo of Biafra merely asked to manage their own affairs, free from persecution and discrimination. The message failed to mention that Nigeria's huge oil reserves, concentrated toward the Bight of Biafra, were a major consideration.

Horror stories circulated about the treatment of Ibo who had earlier been working in northern Nigeria. Two million, it was said, were viciously maltreated, up-rooted, made homeless in a massive displacement of people and a great many died. Now, as the federal noose tightened round the Biafran enclave, the charge was genocide. UNICEF, the Red Cross and other non-governmental organisations did what they could but access was extremely hazardous, by air, by night and readily confused with gun-running. The

International Committee of the Red Cross was given a mandate to coordinate the flow of aid. U Thant obtained agreement from Nigeria's head of state, General Yakubu Gowon, to a small mission 'on humanitarian affairs' to explore what assistance the UN system, could offer, in collaboration with the ICRC (International Committee of the Red Cross). Gussing, knowledgeable about refugees and displaced persons, was chosen also because he was an unassuming man, not a personality likely to attract attention or generate publicity. He was to be accompanied by an assistant, and a secretary. He was entirely satisfied with me, he said at the end of the interview. It was to be a short mission, two or three weeks at most. But we had to be off in forty-eight hours.

Next day I was initiated into the mysteries of an antiquated code machine after being injected in both arms, both buttocks and I forget where else. The nurse issuing anti-malaria and other pills said brightly that she was giving me sufficient for four weeks: 'These missions often run on,' she explained. I packed a suitcase, locked my apartment door and was ready to fly. Only a girl friend seemed upset, principally at having to abandon the Hampton outings she had planned to enliven the summer.

We spent a night in Geneva after calls on the ICRC. The ICRC, staunchly neutral, upholder and champion of the Geneva Conventions, which have done much to mitigate the horrors of warfare, had its headquarters in a venerable, old hotel. As we entered I noticed a plaque commemorating Eglantyne Jebb. She was the remarkable English social reformer and humanitarian who, facing criminal conviction for aiding 'enemy' children, reputedly declared in her defence 'I know no "enemy" under the age of five.' After the first world war she became the founder of Save the Children and was remembered on that wall surrounding the Geneva Conventions' bastion. ICRC protocol was as traditional as its headquarters and as elegant. The chief of protocol introduced himself, 'Borsinger,' he said with a slight bow, and escorted us to a pretty salon.

While we waited briefly Gussing told me that the Borsingers were a well-known Geneva family, eldest sons christened Caspar, Melchior or Balthazar in succession. Fortunately for him, our protocol chief was Caspar. At which he reappeared to conduct us to the Presidential suite for the courtesy call. It produced little of note. The UN was constricted by recognition of Nigeria as a member state. The President was emphatic that the ICRC determined to be absolutely neutral in dealing both with the federal government and Biafra. As commissioner they had appointed August Lindt, former Swiss ambassador to both Washington and Moscow and sometime High Commissioner for Refugees. A distinguished diplomat, Lindt was equally famous for his independence of mind. A bachelor once again after his most recent marriage collapsed when she found he was only marginally related to Lindt chocolate and he discovered she had no connections to Swiss industry. We would meet him shortly in Lagos.

Gus Lindt had his own dedicated aircraft. We flew commercial. Night landings in Lagos were prohibited after a single Biafran overflight into federal airspace made the government wary. We had to land in Accra, in Ghana, before continuing at daybreak next morning. In transit my most onerous responsibility was the mission code machine. Our secretary was a woman and therefore excused from carrying a heavy weight. No one else was authorised. I was charged, like a king's messenger, to keep beside me, though not manacled, a blue and white UN striped diplomatic pouch, officially sealed, which contained the precious and weighty instrument needed to encode and decode confidential communications with New York. I had even been instructed how to operate it in an emergency.

That night, grateful for a few hours in bed, I was woken by hammering on the door. A code cable had come through the UNDP office. Code cables required immediate action. I unravelled the pouch, installed the machine, and woke a disgruntled secretary. The cable, when decoded, proved a repeat of one we had received on leaving Geneva. It provided a telegraphic address for the mission: UNREPNIG. Albeit conforming to usual practice as a logical contraction of 'UN representative to Nigeria', I remonstrated at 'Nig'. I was overruled. Admittedly this was years before 'niggardly' provoked furore in Washington. Gussing slept through it all – lucky man.

Early next day we disembarked at Lagos airport. The 'VIP' lounge, in those days little more than a shack, as many places in Nigeria proved to be, was liberally stocked with beer. Beer flowed from large quart bottles. It seemed impolite not to accept even if it was only eight-thirty in the morning. That remains my most vivid memory of our reception, that and the presence of a charming young man. Lars, first secretary at the Swedish embassy, had come as a gesture to the Swede, Gussing. Sweden's ambassador was home for consultation and Lars remained in charge of their small mission. Normally an insignificant, and not especially agreeable posting for Swedish diplomats, Lagos had assumed importance with Sweden becoming a major supplier of aid. That much aid went to Biafra cost popularity and outside the embassy demonstrators burnt the Swedish flag. Lars was a very effective representative of his country and did much to maintain good relations in a country where those who mattered were young.

Yakubu Gowon was another contemporary. He received Gussing and me later that day. Only in operettas, it was said when Gowon appeared immaculately groomed, in his starched uniform, trousers knife-creased, Sam-Browned, to greet the equally smart young officer who had recently assumed power in Ghana, were heads of state that young, that good-looking, and that beautifully dressed. Gowon was charming. He had a reputation for being likeable; criticism related to his dubious role in the two coups d'etats that had cost hundreds, if not thousands of lives and brought mayhem throughout the military establishment. Although ostensibly mandated to discuss only humanitarian affairs, U Thant expected our mission to evaluate the situation more generally. Was aid allowed to reach the civilian needy, both sides of the fighting; could there be substance to the charge of genocide? The question, needless to say, had to be phrased tactfully. Gowon bristled, recovered his gentle demeanour. He said with solemn conviction that he was fighting to unite Nigeria – the slogan was everywhere 'To keep Nigeria one is the task that must be done' – the war was to bring all the peoples of Nigeria together.

Received by General Gowon, Lagos, Nigeria

Although endorsed not only by the OAU but by the United States, Britain, the Soviet Union and others it was a questionable project. Nigeria as a political entity was the fabrication of British imperialism: smaller tribes apart, it brought together three large and largely incompatible peoples with competing identities not comfortably subsumed into the same nationality. The big three were the Hausa, an Islamic Arab-leaning people feudally ruled who occupied the extensive north, the Yoruba in the west, a more developed people with intellectual and artistic traditions, and the Ibo in the east who had acquired wealth and importance through hard work, discipline and commitment to western education. The northerners, dominant in land area and population, expected commensurate political weight, a privilege resented by the better educated westerners and easterners. The army had been in many respects the most successfully integrated Nigerian institution though the northern region commanded the majority among enlisted men as well as in the ambitious officer corps. The two coups brought into prominence the lack of cross-tribal solidarity in the military.

Gowon himself came from a small middle belt tribe, neither Hausa, Yoruba nor Ibo, but he had grown up among Hausa speakers. He was a Christian. He believed in the justice of his cause and had every intention of seeing it honourably executed. Never, never would he sanction retribution against the Ibo. With one exception. It was hard to forgive Ojukwu, the man who had brought this about, who had divided Nigeria, and turned Nigerian against Nigerian. Ojukwu had been a brother officer; he joined the army after returning from Oxford. Gowon was Sandhurst educated, he reminded us. In later conversations, after he knew that I was an Oxford graduate, he rarely missed the opportunity to emphasise the superior moral and leadership qualities of the Royal Military College. Except for Ojukwu, every Ibo was welcome in Nigeria. Gowon added that for this campaign he had ordered that there be no campaign medals. Brother officers in the mess should never be reminded that they fought against each other.

Gowon's sincerity was hard to question. If not quite the 'simple soldier' he had about him a straightforwardness that convinced. In drafting the report to New York I wanted us to reassure the Secretary-General that Gowon himself wanted reconciliation, genocide was not an official objective. The question, as Gussing and I discussed, was whether Gowon, even if genuinely well-intentioned, had the necessary authority over commanders in the field. The front was divided in three. In the northern sector federal forces had taken the crucial Onitsha bridge over the Niger and were into Enugu, former state and regional capital. The middle-west remained quiescent. Most important was the capture in the south of Port Harcourt, centre of the oil-producing Rivers region.

The 'Black Scorpion', Colonel Benjamin Adekunle, commanded that sector. His brilliance as a military commander was not in doubt, but he was as widely known for his ruthlessness. I was to witness him inspecting rows of wounded soldiers laid out beside an airport runway before evacuation. Every so often, with the heavy ebony stick he carried for swagger cane, he thrashed a bandaged leg or arm, producing agonised shrieks, as he tested, in his own words, for malingerers. Adekunle, with his forces, his war-chest and his reputation for military success and independence, would never be easy to control. The other sector commanders were almost equally independent, if less overtly aggressive. Poor communications rendered tight control still more difficult.

I believed Gowon and wanted to believe that when fighting finished he would have sufficient authority to curb commanders in the field. Not everyone agreed. When eventually the war did end, there was much messy killing but nothing approaching genocide, no mass slaughtering of a defeated enemy. I hope that history gives Gowon some credit. His role in the latest coup that brought him to power remained murky and how he held on to power in the aftermath. He was certainly tougher, more ambitious and complex, than he sometimes appeared. On the other hand the manner of his deposition, the calm surrendering of power, before withdrawing abroad to study says much about the man. Likeable he certainly was. It was for me an advantage to be the same age and, indeed, to share certain ways. This proved helpful when our mission was transformed. Gussing was presented in September 1968 with a note for transmittal to the Secretary-General.

The note advised the Secretary-General of the Nigerian Federal Government's intention to invite independent observers to witness for themselves the conduct of the war – and hopefully confirm that the genocide charge was baseless. The United Kingdom, Canada, Sweden and Poland were being asked, as were the United Nations and the Organisation of African Unity. The idea had purportedly been floated by Britain – the High Commissioner, Sir David Hunt, was knowledgeable and influential. (In retirement he achieved fame as television's mastermind of mastermind.) Observers might be military men, but not necessarily. U Thant's agreement came as no surprise, nor his nomination of Gussing as observer with me as assistant. Gussing was less pleased than I was. For personal reasons he had little wish to extend the mission unduly but a month to six weeks, as envisaged by the Nigerian proposal, did not seem excessive.

Gowon introducing the international observers to his lion cub

The observers had been selected to represent different interests. Britain with manifold links, not least oil-related, was directly involved; Canada came on behalf of north America; Sweden represented neutrality and nordic aid donors; Poland served the interests of the Soviet bloc. The Polish observer was a full colonel, the others were generals; the OAU and the UN appointed civilians. We travelled together. Tours were organised, not very efficiently, to all forward sectors. We saw what we asked to see, and much more by coincidence. 'So bloody inefficient', said one general, 'they couldn't cover up if that's what they intended.' It was not a nice war but war isn't, said another. There was no evidence of systematic killing, of anything that could be considered genocide. The worst, the most heart-rending sight was a ward packed with blankly staring, belly distended, orphaned children suffering from extreme malnutrition. Thankfully, some food and medication were beginning to arrive. In the northern sector and the south fighting continued and we visited more than once. We published detailed reports after every tour. In the middle west there was little action and, after surveying static military positions, the observers were pressed to meet the Oba, ruler of Benin.

When the Portuguese first invaded west Africa and encountered Benin, they were overwhelmed. They discovered a culture more sophisticated in some ways than they had known in Europe. The bronzes, in particular, were remarkable and the Oba's palace, but the society as a whole impressed them deeply. The bronzes, now elsewhere, bought, stolen or removed for safe-keeping, are sole surviving evidence of what had been. Benin declined and what we saw bore little or no resemblance to a nobler past. When the observers were marshalled for their courtesy call, Major-General Alexander, self-appointed spokesman with long experience of soldiering in Africa, explained that some tribute was essential. 'You are supposed to bring a present.' How about a bottle of whiskey? suggested one of the others. Since no one proposed anything better we arrived for our audience at the Oba's palace bearing a bottle of Johnnie Walker.

It was raining as we entered through a long, dim corridor. The rain rattled on the corrugated iron roof. The heavier the rain the more it rattled. Fortunately no discussion was foreseen, only the barest introduction. The Oba, a portly man, with sumptuous raiment draped about him, sat enthroned at one end of his spacious reception chamber. He nodded to each of us in turn before signalling to one of the two retainers, paraded beside him in minimal uniform of near naked splendour, to receive the whiskey bottle. It was placed amid other miscellaneous tribute on a huge table, which occupied the entire central space. We were seated round about. None of us understood the Oba's brief speech, which was not interpreted; and I doubt that he understood a word of what General Alexander said in reply. I passed the time admiring, if admiring is the word, the extraordinary range of bric-a-brac presented to the Oba. Then we trooped out over the beaten earth floor past mud walls whitened in patches here and there. It was still raining as we drove to the airfield at the end of what was intended as our final inspection tour.

Gussing's instincts had been more acute than mine. Once the team of international observers had retoured the battle front in all sectors, observed the conduct of the war, and reported publicly on their failure to find evidence of atrocities, Biafran propaganda reacted. Biafra claimed that federal forces had been under strict orders. Genocide would follow the observers' departure. The Federal government had little choice but ask the observer team to remain. Several of the military observers were changed. The Swedes rotated theirs regularly as did the Canadians.

General Alexander, the British observer, was replaced by Sir Bernard Fergusson, only a Brigadier it was said but with a very distinguished background as a former governor-general of New Zealand. He was known for his ability and experience, his sense of humour, not disliking gin and most of all for his monocle. Sir Bernard was excellent company and I always appreciated being asked to his suite to review the reports he was writing.

Mid-morning, when I came in the door, opened with his politely wondering whether I would not mind pouring him a gin – 'just up to your finger' as I held the tumbler near the middle. On official reports about tours to the front line and conduct of the war his comments were convincing and concise; he was interested but made no attempt to influence what I would be submitting to the UN.

When I knew him better I could not resist mentioning the monocle. That he was pleased to explain. As a young officer cadet he decided that the spectacles he wore for reading, shooting and more were inappropriate to a uniformed officer of the Black Watch, and adopted an eye-glass. The monocle, or eye-glass as he called it, had been with him ever since and he deployed it for an impressive party trick that became his trade-mark. With a jerk of the head he shot the monocle up in the air then caught it again with his eye. The story is told, and it is apparently true, that shortly after Sir Bernard was appointed Governor-General of New Zealand he was invited on an official visit to Australia. The Aussies had wind of this caricature Pommy. The arrival guard of honour all sported monocles. Sir Bernard reviewed the guard punctiliously without batting an eyelid, saluted correctly, and with not even the hint of a smile flicked his monocle into the air and caught it again in his eye. 'Now do that, you bastards!' The Australians loved him.

Sir Bernard Fergusson, he of the monocle

By 1969 Nils Gussing left and I remained as temporary UN representative – with an acting upgrade – and eventually stayed for over a year. Gussing had just gone when the official invitation came to Gowon's wedding. The honour fell to me of representing the UN Secretary-General at a traditional Anglican marriage service in Lagos cathedral. Crowded, humid and extremely hot it was and it came as a relief to move outdoors for a reception in the grounds of Government House. The fine ex-colonial mansion had been well decorated for the occasion. Nigerian men as well as women, opulently dressed in layered acres of brilliantly coloured material, paraded throughout the gardens. Above this magnificent spectacle flew a helicopter drizzling confetti. As the helicopter passed overhead more confetti fell while in the up-draft every bee-hive wig, in the height of fashion on every female head, rose into the air. Some consternation, but mostly amusement; Nigerians have a powerful sense of fun.

Gowon I continued to meet occasionally but I saw another contemporary more often. Yusufu Gobir, permanent secretary at the ministry of defence, had also been to Oxford and at the same time as myself. In Nigeria we became friends. The Ministry of Defence was involved in most matters relating to the international observers, and took responsibility for practical arrangements. Communications in Lagos were appalling. Telephoning rarely worked what with malfunction, flooding, interruption of the line. And having achieved a connection 'is not on seat' was the habitual response. It was more expedient to go to the ministry. Yusufu had given instructions that I should be admitted without prior appointment. Walking into his office one day he glowered for a moment: 'What do all these UN people want? They came to see me two days ago, then again yesterday. Now my secretary says they want another meeting tomorrow. I don't mean you, of course,' and he smiled warmly. I asked him who these 'UN people' were. He hardly knew, so I turned to the secretary. 'Yes, they are all UN people,' she said, 'UNICEF, WHO, World Food Programme and ...' she could not remember the others and went to look. To me Yusufu said: 'Why can't they come at the same time? It would help us understand their different roles and how they mesh, if they do. And don't they realise we're busy, we're fighting a war.' A Damascene moment for me. In any disaster situation, natural or man-made, it obviously made sense for UN organisations to function in a coordinated way, to meet jointly and present their case together. It could be as important for them as for the receiving government.

I had accepted with alacrity when asked to remain in Nigeria after Gussing left. On mission I discovered that the UN mattered, and the individual's contribution mattered. Apart from reports on tours to the war zone, investigating any reported incident, and constant dealings with agency, government and non-governmental representatives on increasing humanitarian assistance and improving ways for its delivery, there was a weekly political and situation report for the Secretary-General to be drafted. What I was doing felt significant – to Nigeria and to the UN. This was a far cry from the nine-to-five relative irrelevance of work in New York. Or so it seemed to me. I was delighted to continue, with just one modest condition. Having departed at forty-eight hours notice on a mission of three to four weeks, I was asking, after six months, to be recalled for consultations. Two days would suffice. The compelling need, less than to consult or be consulted, was to put my belongings in storage and vacate the apartment; my lease was due to expire.

A couple of intense days achieved their objective. Only much later did I pay a price for precipitate storage: two beloved Braque prints, a Rouault and a museum worthy headhunter's shield from Sarawak failed to reappear when I eventually moved back to a new apartment in New York. I was heard in the Secretary-General's office; others too listened respectfully to my assessment of Nigeria-Biafra. Several colleagues said how much they envied me the experience. One of them also insisted that I call on Martin Hill, the Assistant-Secretary-General for Inter-Agency Affairs and I was unsure why. Mr Hill was not officially concerned with Africa. But as a UN system man he followed the agencies and their work. He seemed very pleasant, though with no specific reason to be interested in meeting me. It came as a surprise when weeks after returning to Nigeria I received his cable.

He invited me to become his Special Assistant. The explanation followed months later. Martin had been actively recruiting a new special assistant. The chosen candidate was a Trinidadian diplomat, able and ambitious, whose ambition prevailed over judgment. He insisted on appointment as a P5 and he and his mission lobbied intensively. It was the era when non-whiteness emerged as a distinct advantage. The appointments and promotion board was disposed to favour his appointment until Personnel bureaucratically ruled that the post was classified P3/4 and could not be reclassified at the higher level. The Trinidadian was hoist with his own petard. He had insisted, thinking this a compelling argument, that he would accept only at P5. Martin Hill, brusquely deprived of his candidate and needing an urgent decision, chose me.

12 Disaster relief and Bahrain's independence

INTER-AGENCY AFFAIRS covered a range of responsibilities. These included the preparation and submission to ECOSOC and the General Assembly of reports on activities involving UN system coordination. Assistance in response to natural disasters was one. The Secretary-General had at his disposal a discretionary fund from which he could contribute token aid to countries afflicted. The contribution was essentially symbolic, intended as seed money.

When Martin asked that I draft the routine report, I described to him my Nigerian experience. I explained the self-evident problems confronting governments, especially the less developed, during crises when their structures were disrupted, in having to cope with multiple international organisations, often unfamiliar, as well as donor governments and non-governmental organisations. Coordinated action would be to everyone's advantage. It would make the best use of resources as well as benefiting the disaster-struck country if UN organisations operated together as a team. I proposed including this as a novel element in the report. Martin listened. All his life he had been a bureaucrat and bureaucrats are not programmed to take unauthorised initiative. He would have a word with Harry Labouisse.

Labouisse was head of UNICEF. UNICEF had played an important and effective role in bringing aid to Nigeria-Biafra, as I had been telling Martin. Labouisse may have been less extrovert, perhaps less charismatic, than his successor Jim Grant – with his oral re-hydration tablets constantly to hand – but he was as effective. He had earned the world's respect for UNICEF. Like the best leaders he knew how to listen. At our meeting Martin proposed that I speak. Little P3s were not in the habit of speaking in the presence of Assistant and Under-Secretary-Generals; they took notes. Labouisse nodded. I recounted the Nigerian experience and explained my thinking. Martin mentioned the routine report due for the General Assembly, wondering whether it could be appropriate to build in my ideas. Labouisse thought definitely 'yes'. With that endorsement, Martin had no hesitation in urging me to go ahead.

An outline was taking shape in my mind, though I had yet to start writing, when Martin Hill summoned me. He had been asked by the thirty-eighth floor to release me for a mission. A brief mission, he was assured, early in the year. That was everything he knew. It was all very secret. He was as reluctant to say more as he was to release me. But he felt he had no choice, on the assumption, that was, that I wanted to go. Of course, I did. On the thirty-eighth floor, in the offices of Ralph Bunche, I was sworn to secrecy. The Secretary-General planned sending a small mission to Bahrain in 1970: his representative, a deputy and one political officer plus minimal support staff. The representative, Vittorio Winspeare Guicciardi, a distinguished Italian diplomat recently named UN Director-General at Geneva, had specifically asked for me on the team. I had never met Mr Winspeare, or so I thought before remembering the briefest of courtesy calls when en route to Nigeria with Nils Gussing.

Those Nigerian situation reports that I conscientiously drafted week in week out, doubting anyone read them, had been copied to Winspeare as the UN official link with the ICRC. He had enquired who wrote them and that was the man he wanted for his mission. It could have been a pastiche of Winston Churchill having admired wartime reports from Washington inviting the author I. Berlin to 10 Downing Street only to imagine his guest at luncheon was Irving, not Isaiah. Fortunately, at the UN there was no other E. Jensen on record.

Whatever I had the potential to contribute it was not knowledge of Bahrain. I knew little enough about the Persian Gulf beyond the announcement that British forces were being withdrawn from the area. That was the catalyst. Bahrain had been under British protection for years while the Royal Navy dominated gulf waters. In the past it had been ruled by the Persian empire. Iran still claimed it and in the Iranian parliament two seats remained vacant for delegates from Bahrain. The ruling dynasty in Bahrain, the El-Khalifa, were not Iranian, neither Farsi-speaking nor Shia; they were Arabs, Arabic-speaking and Sunni and lived conveniently cheek by jowl with Saudi Arabia. A causeway linked the two with Saudi oil flowing out through Bahraini refineries.

The Shah of Iran, whatever his shortcomings in domestic policy, showed political vision. Impossible as it was for him simply to surrender Iran's ancient, historic claim, he also recognised that force used in asserting the Iranian claim could only lead to war, but force was an inevitable consequence were Iran to impose sovereignty over the emirate. At a press conference during an official visit abroad he fielded questions about Bahrain. Without yielding on principle Iran, he announced, would abide by the recommendations of the UN Secretary-General on the island's future, as endorsed by the Security Council.

U Thant had agreed to exercise his good offices. It had to be strictly confidential. He had no specific mandate from the Security Council, no formal authority, no budget. The US and the UK stood solidly behind him, but the French were not fully briefed and the Soviets were deliberately left out of the loop. This was the cold war, the very cold war. What suited one side, antagonised the other. In the Gulf the pieces were ill assorted. Iran, at that time, was in the western camp, Arab nations generally closer to the Soviet Union, but Bahrain pro-west. U Thant's decision was brave. He needed a report to the Security Council that could satisfy Bahrain and appease the Arabs without antagonising Iran, which should make it impossible for any power to block in the Council. The mission had to be in place before it might be disrupted by lobbying and interest groups. Hence the secrecy. In charge, that master of discreet diplomacy, was Ralph Bunche.

He flew to Geneva over Christmas to brief Winspeare in person. No correspondence to leak. On my appointment Bunche assembled me in his office with F.T. Liu, his long serving Director who was to be the deputy, and Brian Urquhart, the only other person to know about the mission. I would be the political officer. Liu and I were to fly first to Geneva for preliminary consultation with Winspeare before continuing to Bahrain as an advance party a day or so before his arrival. Our bookings had been made under assumed names. In no circumstances was I to tell anyone. Bunche's humour surfaced only at the mission's cable address GOMB. GOMB was the acronym for the Good Offices Mission, Bahrain. Even that had to be confidential for the moment.

Meeting Winspeare in Geneva was focussed and agreeable. He was superbly briefed, confident in what the mission should achieve, precise in every instruction. F.T. Liu, he confirmed as deputy, I was head of chancery. Incidentally, he wished to be addressed as Mr Winspeare, not Guicciardi, which no one pronounced correctly, and it was a function of mine to make that known. Neither Liu nor I should speak to the press; he hoped we could avoid any media interest until after we had landed in Manama. Thank goodness, he added, it was not summer; summer months in the Gulf were impossibly hot and humid. With that we departed accompanied by an administrative assistant and security officer; a UN interpreter was to join us in the region.

At the airport I acquired a bottle of whiskey. It seemed prudent to have provision in an Islamic country. Then just before landing F.T.Liu decided alcohol might jeopardise our mission and asked me to jettison the bottle. I presented it, elegantly, to the prettiest of the cabin crew; she was delighted and surprised. Our hotel in Manama had a fully stocked bar. Bahrain had no prohibition. Of our two Bahraini liaison officers I became particular friends with Ali Mahrooz and Ali was always generous with excellent wine when he invited us to dine, more then once on 'lobestar'. Though that gives a distorted view of the mission.

Winspeare with his team in Manama, Bahrain

We worked hard, long hours determined to produce a report that would convince the Security Council and enable Bahrain to advance peacefully to full independence. Everything was complicated or sensitive or both. Even geographical terminology. The Gulf was known through history as the Persian Gulf. This was on the official maps and used by Iran. The Arab countries in and surrounding the Gulf insisted on calling it the Arabian Gulf. Correspondence addressed 'Bahrain, Persian Gulf' was returned, marked 'address unknown'. It was no help arguing that gulfs were traditionally called by the name of where they led to. This became seriously contentious. The Iranians maintained that the official report should refer unequivocally to the 'Persian Gulf', that was what it was, and had always been called. We could not risk a report insufficiently sympathetic to Iranian sensibilities since the

Shah needed to convince his people. The Bahrainis, and their Arab friends, were equally adamant that they would never accept reference to the Gulf as Persian, it was Arabic.

It distressed me that such an issue, of prestige but prestige based only on a name, and the name of a international waterway, should be given that importance. The compromise eventually accepted, largely because both sides welcomed the thrust of our report, had reference in the text neutered to 'The Gulf' and a UN map attached. The official UN map, which included a disclaimer, had 'Persian Gulf' appear in such tiny print as to be barely legible. The findings achieved precedence.

In Bahrain Winspeare concurred in consulting the population through local associations, known as clubs. While not pure democracy, it was a channel to popular opinion. Had 'votes' been evenly balanced this approach would not have been acceptable, but a majority view prevailed sufficiently for the Secretary-General to advise the Council that Bahrain aspired to full independence as an Arab state. Looking back we probably have to accept that the procedure was rigged, though the outcome was right, for the time. The Shia majority of the population may have been more sympathetic to Iran than the Sunni Arab rulers wanted the world to know but our 'findings' enabled a durable, peaceful solution when the alternative was probably war.

As the mission prepared to depart our interpreter, a Lebanese, announced excitedly that the Bahraini government wished to present us all with gold Rolex watches. You could see his fleshy Levantine face salivating at the prospect. I seldom saw Winspeare angry, but he reacted instantly and with force. In no circumstances, in no circumstances whatsoever, was any member of his mission to accept a gift. It was contrary to UN regulations, and, even more important, it would be seen as bribery in a case where nothing must be allowed to challenge us as scrupulously neutral. He glowered at the interpreter, who flushed, winced. Poor fellow, he badly wanted that gold Rolex. To compensate, on our last afternoon, Winspeare agreed to visit a goldsmith in the souk; he and others might wish to purchase small presents to take home. Ali Mahrooz, who escorted us, kept urging me to buy. I had no one at the time who merited jewellery but under pressure I bought for my sister a modest ring set with a pearl. Bahrain had genuine pearl fishers and it was real albeit small.

Years later I stopped over in Bahrain, the only time I have since been back. Ali, at the airport in the small hours insisted that we lunch next day before my onward flight. The mission had been a great success for the country, he said. I said how much I had enjoyed being part of it. We reminisced. He wanted to know why on earth I had been so reluctant to buy anything in the souk.

At the time I had no one special to buy for, I explained. Hadn't I understood that the prices we were asked to pay were only half true value? The Bahrainis had arranged with the jeweller to indemnify him. I had no idea, I said. The interpreter did, said Ali.

The mission concluded in 1970 not in Bahrain but New York. The Secretary-General's report came before the Council in open session. By then both French and Soviets were comprehensively informed. Miffed though they were at being side-lined, neither had interest in sabotaging an outcome favoured by allies. Despite nerves, earlier reservations and some unabated tension, the Council voted unanimously to adopt the Secretary-General's recommendations. Rejoicing, one permanent member broke into verse – the only such poet-tasting occasion of which I am aware. Lord Caradon, the UK ambassador, read out loud the rhymes he had written in praise of those responsible, from U Thant and Bunche to Winspeare – 'we're proud he has an English name'; Hugh Caradon's reputation as a man and a diplomat ensured an appreciative reception. So successful was the mission, so discreet its conduct, so orderly and peaceful the subsequent transfer of power that the media took little notice.

Next morning, back in Inter-Agency Affairs, Winspeare arrived to thank Martin Hill for having loaned me. On his way out he passed my little office next door. Would I be interested in working in Geneva, he asked, when his present chef de cabinet retired the following year? Martin had already told me of his own expected retirement in a year's time and I said 'yes'. In the doorway Winspeare glanced encouragingly at my name plate: 'Too many "assistants" here, I think, don't you?' Before his return to Geneva U Thant gave a luncheon in Winspeare's honour. To my delight I was also invited – 'you were mentioned in dispatches' Winspeare said. Lunch in the Secretary-General's private dining-room was informal, relaxed and un-businesslike. U Thant drank his favourite pina colada and chatted casually to the six of us round the table. Conversation was light-hearted and I remember best the agreeable atmosphere.

As Martin Hill approached retirement, having experienced at first hand the demise of the League, holding action during the war years and the UN from its earliest days, Colombia and Princeton universities both invited him. He was to write, to tell it 'like it was'. Martin declined. After forty years drafting UN documents and official correspondence, he said he could only write one way. Though he enjoyed telling stories, many of which he told me. There were several about the first Secretary-General Trygve Lie, who was notoriously puritanical despite occasional alter egoish behaviour.

An incident in the youthful secretariat provoked consternation in certain quarters. A security guard on fire-alarm duty had chanced upon a man and a woman, desk-top, in flagrante, and reported it. Lie, profoundly indignant, convoked his senior staff. He understood that the couple had been discovered in the translation service. Lie, in his most censorious manner, demanded to know in which language division. An awkward silence followed. Then Languier, the French Assistant Secretary-General, spoke. 'I claim the honour for France,' he said. And everyone laughed – except Lie. A complex man he must have been; in Geneva he went incognito to a night-club using an assumed name; to complete his disguise as Rodney Witherspoon, English gent abroad, Lie wore a heavy tweed suit. He must have been supremely noticeable in any Geneva night-club. No wonder the Swiss police were concerned whether there could be a security issue, Martin added with a laugh.

Meanwhile, at the General Assembly, our disaster relief report caused few ripples. It did induce several governments and some organisations to reflect on the desirability of a common front and common approach in the aftermath of disaster. The Economic and Social Council voted for a first step preliminary report on 'Assistance in Cases of Natural Disaster'. In 1970 the earthquake in Peru and appalling floods in the Bay of Bengal with great loss of life generated public and media awareness, and gave impetus to our proposals. A comprehensive report for submission to ECOSOC in 1971 offered scope to infiltrate what I had long considered especially important: the additional words 'and other disaster situations'. The international community, its states and organisations, was receiving a clear mandate to be better prepared, to work more effectively together and more promptly to help the needy in all disasters, even political crises and civil war. Both the Americans and the British were interested.

UN documents are not attributed; they appear as reports of the Secretary-General. Martin Hill appreciated the warm commendation offered him on the disaster assistance proposals but made no secret of my authorship. Hence a call from the US permanent mission shortly after our arrival in Geneva for the ECOSOC summer session. The ambassador, from New York, over for the formal opening, wished to invite me for lunch. He suggested an Italian restaurant in the old town. I had no problem with Italian food and Geneva old town was charming.

The ambassador was there to greet me, had I had any difficulty in finding the restaurant (the difficulty lay in finding somewhere to park), was this a good table, would I like to take my coat off – it was hot? Relaxed and easy, he could not have been more agreeable. Did I want some wine? This was the time when Americans were emerging from two dry martinis, by way of spritzers, to water with lunch. I said 'yes, please'. George Bush, *père*, drank water. His government needed some clarification about the disaster relief recommendations, which in general they supported. I was pleased to respond. We talked of that, then other things before parting as friends. Not for one second did it cross my mind that this tall, amiable, straightforward, not markedly perceptive or articulate man would one day become president of the United States. I met George Bush once again, many years later, when he came to the UN as US president soon after being sick on a state visit to Japan.

ECOSOC voted in favour of our proposals. A disaster relief coordinator would be appointed, donor governments and organisations would commit to better coordination, and disaster prone nations be helped to improve disaster preparedness and coordination of their own responsibilities when disaster struck. Subject to General Assembly budgetary approval the Office of a UN Disaster Relief Coordinator was born. Martin Hill was encouraged, before he himself retired, to indicate a suitable first coordinator: a man of stature, experience and with the energy to galvanise others in making the new office and its ambitious functions effective.

Kurt Waldheim was elected on his birthday 21 December 1971 to succeed U Thant as UN Secretary-General. I remember the date because Waldheim and I shared a birthday. I like to think that all resemblance ends there. He was an arrogant man, with overweening ambition, political to his finger-tips. Even before the start pistol it showed. To become Disaster Relief Coordinator Martin Hill had sounded and obtained the agreement of Henrik Beer, the Secretary-General of the League of Red Cross Societies, a man widely admired, energetic, and immensely knowledgeable about disaster assistance, ideal for the post. U Thant chose not to name him immediately only because he thought so significant a new appointment should be left to his successor. Waldheim instead picked an obscure Turkish diplomat, whose principal qualification was having a non-Turkish partner of many years of whom he wished to make an honest woman; Turkish diplomats were not allowed to remain in their foreign service if married to a foreigner. Waldheim was asked this favour by Bayulkin, Foreign Minister of Turkey and former colleague at the UN, and seems to have believed that such an accommodating gesture would enable him to resolve the dispute over Cyprus. It did nothing for disaster relief.

To help instal the new disaster relief office was one of my tasks when I arrived in Geneva to take up the post of Chef de Cabinet to the Director-General in a somewhat grander setting than the premises I had known in

New York. The silver corridor where the directorate had offices was very well-appointed at the heart of the Palais des Nations. The Palais had grandeur, it was pretentious, a vast monument set on a hill overlooking the Lake of Geneva. Building had been completed when the League of Nations was already failing. Hitler had come to power, Mussolini had not been prevented from invading Abyssinia despite Emperor Haile Selasse's impassioned appeal to the League, Germany was not the only nation to be actively rearming. Chamberlain's pledge of 'peace in our time' convinced only those who remembered the ghastliness of trench warfare and refused to imagine another war. When Hitler marched the League was powerless. History lived on in the Palais.

13 The Palais, East Pakistan into Bangladesh

THE PALAIS NEVER FULLY ESCAPED from its era and the collapse of the League. That was one reason the successor organisation, the United Nations, went to New York; another, more important, was to tie in the United States, which had not been a member of the League. Reminders cluttered the Palais, not ugly but as lingering reminders of their time. The oak tree in the grounds donated by Latvia, no more an independent state; a charming 'salon Tcheque' with no relevance to communist Czechoslovakia; a tapestry, source not given, of St Martin giving half his cloak to a poor man (was half sharing symbolic?); fine low relief carving by Eric Gill in 'Thou fingering me God' homage to Michelangelo with man 'set above the beasts' in Latin; theatrical murals by J.M. Sert, who had worked on Diaghilev's productions, with columns of bronze and gold. Sert's technical brilliance in painting the arched ceiling of the Council chamber impressed more than any allegorical significance. I never tired of trying to decipher his miraculous handling of perspective – the towers and turrets all remained upright as you passed from one side to the other – as an antidote to the drowsiness inevitably induced by boring speeches especially in summer when it was hot and close.

July was typically hot and close when the Palais took into use four new large conference rooms all fully air-conditioned. A few delegates complained at the lack of windows, only artificial light, but most complaints centred on another innovation. It was decided, following a World Health Organization initiative, to ban smoking. No smoking would be permitted in any of the new air-conditioned conference chambers, a more revolutionary measure than it appears today. Reluctant compliance became the rule. Until the summer session of the Economic and Social Council.

I was accosted by a mini delegation: the secretary of ECOSOC and the Council's president. The president that year was a Brazilian, who compensated for being physically small by projecting an enlarged sense of his own importance. He puffed incessantly, blew smoke about him, and announced that it was inconceivable that he preside over the Council's deliberations without smoking. The more I explained about WHO policy, their recommendation that conference rooms be smoke-free, the more the little man chafed, and puffed. He stormed off stating there would be no meeting, no splendid inaugural session of the Council in its new chamber, if he was not enabled to smoke. Dog-like the secretary, who was a contemporary I knew well from New York, followed with an embarrassed slightly superior smile saying he pitied me. I am almost ashamed to admit that I did order a single ash-tray for the podium to underpin Brazilian self-importance. The grand opening went ahead in the Secretary-General's presence.

Ordering ash-trays was, happily, peripheral to my real work which focussed on political events and special missions. Most important were the middle east discussions in the presence of Kissinger in 1973, the talks during the 1974 Turkish invasion of Cyprus presided over by Jim Callaghan, the missions to India, Pakistan and Bangladesh when East Pakistan ceased to be, and to East Timor. The middle east talks were adjourned just short of Christmas Eve. When the bugle sounded summoning me to the Indian subcontinent it was Boxing Day 1971. Why was it missions happened at Christmastide. In many crises the Council is unable or unwilling to agree on action to be taken. Asking the Secretary-General to send a high-level mission counts as acting, sometimes useful as a delaying tactic, and especially convenient when Council members plan to be on holiday. Decisions can await their return, the Secretary-General's report, and developments on the ground.

Bangladesh, still officially known as East Pakistan, had broken from the West and, with the support of India, declared independence in December 1971. The bitter struggle in Bengal generated massive humanitarian problems. India was having to feed and shelter Bengali refugees, who had escaped into Indian territory in their hundred thousand, and could not continue to do so. This was the compelling crisis, the immediate reason prompting Security Council action. Bangladesh, though freed of military conflict, had no reserves to reabsorb the refugees, lacked resources, competent administration, political leadership. In Dhaka there was an additional problem of desperate Biharis. Amputated Pakistan, West Pakistan, having been embarrassingly humiliated, needed the return of its army and most senior officers, held prisoner-of-war by India, and to recover dignity.

The Secretary-General named Winspeare his representative with me to accompany him. Together we travelled to Delhi before the year end 1971.

Given the heightened sensitivities all round it was felt that a discreet mission would be more effective. Our mandate was vague, also vaguely comprehensive: to be helpful in addressing humanitarian issues within UN competence. The Indians needed us least. What they wanted was for UNHCR to finance, organise and repatriate as expeditiously as possible the Bengali refugees. The minister received us courteously but left serious talk to his most senior official, D.P. Dhar.

Controlling relief flight from Geneva to Bay of Bengal

Dhar asked politely: 'What can we do for you?' He sat back behind his desk, a spare man in an exceedingly spare office. I had noticed on entering, instead of other decoration on the wall, a typed list of the room's modest inventory. Every item was listed and given a number, even the wooden foot-rest visible beneath the desk was labelled F/R in white paint and numbered. Austerity determined the agenda. Winspeare, the experienced diplomat, steered Dhar into talking.

Dhar mentioned the refugee issue, the impossible burden it had been and continued to be for India. This was surely a responsibility of the international community. Expenditure exceeded lachs by the million. The rights of these Bengali refugees had long been discussed 'threadbare' – his word. They had to go back. They could not remain in India. These were people, Muslims, who had originally and deliberately chosen Islamic Pakistan in preference to India. Winspeare asked about prisoners-of-war. That was a matter for India and

Pakistan, Dhar maintained. International involvement would not be helpful, thank you very much.

We tried discussing the situation more generally. Bangladesh, as Indians now openly referred to the place we had still to call East Pakistan, was highly unstable, 'I am nearly using the word chaotic,' Dhar said. 'The Bengalis, even our Bengalis …' and he raised both eyebrows without finishing the sentence. They badly needed leadership. Dhar brightened as he said it. 'There is way you can be helpful.' If we could help have Sheikh Mujibur Rahman released from detention in Pakistan and returned to Bangladesh. It was the extraordinary election result that had precipitated the current crisis. Mujib's Awami League had won an overwhelming majority, which posed an insuperable challenge to any common political structure. Dhar summoned his assistant, Dixit; 'Mr Dick-Shit is giving you all statistics.' Winspeare and I smiled, politely, before leaving.

Britain, we knew from the ambassador, stood ready to fly Mujib to Dhaka, requiring clearance, but also Pakistani agreement, which was not forthcoming. Switzerland had generously made available to our mission a small executive aircraft. From what we were told, this was the only plane authorised to fly direct from Delhi to Islamabad. Islamabad, where we landed next day, was a sad, dejected place. Laid out to become a modern capital city with wide roads, avenues, all at right angles to each other, it remained at the planning stage. With few buildings complete it had the air of a project abandoned before being realised. It further depressed the mood. Inglorious capitulation in East Pakistan and the imprisonment of its proud army – Muslims from a warrior tradition – was deeply embarrassing, shameful.

If they had lost a war they had lost none of their crisp, military smartness. Our driver was meticulously uniformed and correct. So correct that at every intersection when the light showed green, he stopped, looked both ways, before driving on. There was no one about, not a vehicle in sight. Then I noticed that he drove straight through red lights. The third or fourth time I could not help asking whether green had come to mean stop. 'No, Sir, no, but is always some damn-fool driver driving through on red.'

Even the diplomatic community seemed uncertain how to proceed, reduced, numbed. I speculated how the current situation was being assessed and reported to capitals, how many if any were claiming to have predicted this turn of events. The British ambassador had us to dinner with little news to convey beyond confirming that he was no longer High Commissioner; Pakistan left the Commonwealth immediately Britain recognised Bangladesh. On the subject of Mujib he reaffirmed Britain's readiness to fly him to Dhaka a soon as he could be released. This was a matter of high priority. He urged us to add our UN voice to the cause when meeting President Bhutto.

The audience with Bhutto was set for the following morning. He lived grandly, in a mansion which had once been the residence of an imperial general, and all accoutrements reflected its importance. Sentries guarded the impressive entrance. They saluted our arrival smartly, checked the driver, checked the passengers, VWG and myself, repeated names, saluted again before authorising a lesser rank to open the fine wrought iron gates. We advanced along an imposing tree-lined drive toward the main building. Before a palatial flight of steps the car stopped. Forward stepped an Aide de Camp to open the passenger door. Courteous and formal he escorted us up the steps, through great doors, into a vast chamber. The President will be with you shortly, he said, and retired. We were left to admire the surroundings more than long enough to appreciate Bhutto's greatness.

When he came, he entered from the far end. Two flunkeys flung open double doors at the same moment. Bhutto made his entrance dressed in the height of fashion, contemporary western fashion. He wore a double-breasted, multiple buttoned suit, and a tie knotted expansively. 'Good morning,' he said. 'Welcome to Pakistan.' Like Gladstone, who was accused of speaking to Queen Victoria as if addressing a public meeting, Bhutto delivered an oration. At considerable length he justified Pakistan's action in the East. He blamed the Awami League and its leader Mujibur Rahman for propagating unrest, guerrilla warfare, and the break-up of Pakistan. In all he had to say there was nothing contrite and little conciliatory.

Winspeare, responding, was brief. His comments on events were not wanted, anyway. He concentrated on humanitarian issues: the refugees in India, the fate of the Biharis, and the case of Mujibur Rahman, imprisoned in Pakistan. If a UN aircraft were desired to repatriate him to Dhaka, which might be a very helpful move, indeed this could be a distinctively statesmanlike gesture on the part of Pakistan, Winspeare was sure we could help – the British had already offered, we knew, of course, but wondered about lingering irritation at Britain's hurried recognition of Bangladesh. The refugees were a problem for India and Dhaka, Bhutto maintained, they had provoked it, they were responsible for the situation and its consequences. The Biharis, well, they were Bihari and Bihar was remote from West Pakistan. In any event the West lacked resources to absorb them. On Mujib he offered little. We surmised that he was moving towards a solution but was not yet willing openly to commit himself. He thanked us for the offer of assistance.

An exploratory visit to Dhaka proved how grim the situation was. The airport had been heavily bombed: the runways fissured, water standing in craters and surface cracking made landing impossible for larger aircraft and dangerous for all. We flew in by a small STOL – short take-off and landing – plane with an adventurous pilot, to land safely in a remote corner. The hotel where we stayed was depleted of everything, including guests. Winspeare was offered a choice of suites; they were all the same, poorly maintained. Then seeing a kitchenette, he said cheerfully: 'We can make spaghetti.' I thought that was why we had an Italian with us, I said, and at once wondered whether I had overstepped the mark, but he took it in good part. Though he did not propose cooking when that evening we prepared for dinner.

We dined alone in the hotel dining-room on the only dish available. I do not remember what, except it was unappetising. 'A little wine might have helped' said Winspeare, at which we both realised it was New Year's Eve. 'Then we must have a bottle of wine,' he said and called the waiter. 'No, Sir, very sorry, Sir,' said the waiter, 'there is no wine.' The head waiter, the only other person in the room, overheard. He would have a further look, he volunteered. After some considerable interval he returned with an indifferent red. 'This is last only bottle we have in hotel,' he had found it forgotten in a storage room. Winspeare glanced at his watch; it was ten o'clock. He wondered whether we had to wait till midnight to drink the appropriate toast. The room was dimly lit, the only company two miserable looking waiters. 'It's already midnight somewhere,' I said. We drank to the New Year wherever – without really savouring the ghastly wine.

As well we had an early night because next day we faced Mirpur and Mohamedpur. Mirpur and Mohamedpur had previously been pleasant suburban districts. They were transformed into concentration camps. Here the large Bihari population was cantoned. Biharis, at Indian independence, split between the Hindu Biharis who chose to remain Indian and the Muslims who opted to join Islamic Pakistan, in their case neighbouring East Pakistan. East Pakistan was almost entirely Bengali. The Biharis, albeit fellow Muslims, were not Bengali speaking and rarely identified with Bengali culture. They aligned themselves with Urdu speaking administrators assigned from the West. Many were well educated, and the Biharis prospered, commonly associated with non-Bengalis in positions of influence. They had few friends when West Pakistani forces and administrators withdrew, defeated, and Bengali resistance fighters took power. Outcast, unwanted, initially for their own protection, later for control, they were herded together in once prosperous suburbs.

Winspeare and I were provided with a chauffeur-driven car and an escort. The escort comprised an open lorry with assorted armed men in the back. We drove in convoy through human misery. Rubbish, rubble, remains were everywhere. Here and there lay a body, dying or dead. Sewage flowed and stank. Our air-conditioned car inhaled the stench, and it was better with the windows open till people began poking in bony, scabby arms as we passed slowly around potholes and whatever had been discarded mid-street. From a longish road we turned into a square, where the inmates were corralled. They surged towards us away from the cistern truck dispensing its meagre ration of water. The driver stopped.

The moment he stepped from the car Winspeare was accosted. An elderly man, claiming to speak on behalf of all those thronging round him, asked that we receive a petition. Another man pressed forward, waving a sealed envelope. Shouting through a loud-hailer he delivered an impassioned speech, not in English. The great mass of people moved excitedly. The original spokesman, in good English, explained that we could see for ourselves the appalling conditions to which the Biharis had been reduced, through no fault of their own. Minimal food distribution and a cistern truck delivering inadequate water barely kept the healthy alive; the old and children were dying of malnutrition and starvation; illness was spreading. The UN had to help – which he repeated again, loudly, in his own language. He insisted that Mr Winspeare, as the Secretary-General's representative, call the Secretary-General immediately, make him promise to intervene.

Winspeare promised to apprise the Secretary-General fully of the situation, how grave it was. He would do all he could to bring help. That was not enough, not nearly enough. The spokesman insisted on action. They would hold us till the Secretary-General responded. The man with the loud-hailer thrust it into Winspeare's face saying he had to address the crowd and endorse his commitment. Winspeare, made very uncomfortable by this physical assault, spoke into the mouthpiece and his voice boomed into the crowd. But he could only pledge to ensure that the UN Secretary-General was made fully aware of the Biharis' plight. As he turned back towards the car, a great mass of people surged forwards, waving and shouting. 'Let's go,' said Winspeare sharply to me, and urged the driver on.

We had driven barely two or three yards, and very slowly, when a man prostrated himself before the front wheel. The driver, a Bengali, was soaked in sweat, you could smell it, you could see beads on his face, his hands; he was terrified of being lynched. There we were. Blocked. Unable to move, surrounded by desperate people. Beyond, some fifty yards ahead, in the escort vehicle our complement of scruffy Bengali soldiers stood holding up weapons. (Was there not a rule that a security escort must always stay close?) My God, I thought, don't let them shoot. If they as much as fire warning shots into the air, there will be total pandemonium, and anything could happen. That was when I did something risky.

I got out of the car, though Winspeare said stay, and instructed the driver to follow right behind me. Having dragged to one side the prostrate man who lay limply, I started to walk slowly but determinedly ahead. I advanced, less like Stephenson leading 'The Rocket' than Moses dividing the waters. Little by very little the crowd divided, ceased harassing me, then drew back as the car inched forward. Perhaps they realised gradually that holding us served no purpose. A gap developed. I jumped back in as we drove off, cautiously but uninterrupted, till we reached the escort vehicle and were able to leave the camp. Winspeare reported in the strongest possible terms to New York on the Biharis and their situation. These wretched people had alienated India, by leaving for a Muslim homeland in East Pakistan, and offended the Bengalis, by siding with Urdu speakers from the West, and West Pakistan had no place for them. They had nowhere left to turn.

Sheikh Mujibur Rahman was released from detention and arrived in Dhaka to a hero's welcome. His Awami League had triumphed with the support of an overwhelming majority, the dominating Urdu-speaking West Pakistanis had been humiliated and expelled from Bangladesh, land of the Bengalis, at last his people were truly independent. Mujibur Rahman identified with 'his' people to an exceptional degree. Everything was his: roads, bridges, hospitals, schools.

Mujib had nothing in common with Bhutto, political ambition apart. If Bhutto was elegantly dressed, westernised, oozing self-confidence in a sophisticated setting, Mujib was in many respects the reverse. He occupied a modest ex-colonial villa where a front room served to receive callers. Like patients in a provincial dentist's or a doctor's waiting-room people sat round walls, shuffling occasionally, clearing their throat, some talking, some in silence – there were no magazines – without apparent organisation beyond the individual who ushered petitioners in from outside. We had passed a sentry on duty by the garden gate, casually uniformed as from an army surplus store, slumped over his rifle. No smart salute as he nodded us through to where Winspeare and I joined others waiting.

Mujib emerged from an adjoining door. Well built, with handsome features and a clipped moustache, his dhoti dangling loose about him, he made a theatrical entrance in his style. He opened wide his arms, priest-like, and nodded benignly at all present. He spoke briefly to someone before inviting us to his sanctuary. His English was not on a par with Bhutto's; in that as in everything else there was about him a homespun quality, which he liked to exaggerate. He was the father of his people, yet always one of them, one with them. When he spoke of past events, he identified himself with Bangladesh, its population, even its infrastructure. Several times he accused the Pakistanis: 'They have destroyed my bridges, they have destroyed my roads, they have destroyed my …' in an endless inventory of everything belonging to the country.

Bangladesh had been born, but disinherited, penniless. This was his appeal for aid. The return of ten million refugees would be enormously costly for the new nation, and to rebuild all that had been destroyed – he quoted from the listing. He counted on the international community. The exchange of prisoners was not his concern. As for the Biharis, they had chosen not to integrate, they had not made any effort to speak Bengali, they had aligned themselves with West Pakistanis, they had brought on themselves their predicament. They should be repatriated to West Pakistan. Was there no possibility of absorbing them into Bangladeshi society? Winspeare asked. Mujib said only if they were to become loyal citizens, committed to Bangladesh, mastering Bengali, in a tone implying that as inconceivable.

The Bihari issue proved one of the most intractable with which I have been involved; the Secretary-General refused to make it a priority concern.

14 Waldheim, secretary-general, and East Timor

WITH WALDHEIM IT WAS ALWAYS POLITICS, especially politics relevant to his person. But whatever the motivation, his capacity for hard work impressed me on his regular visits to Geneva. Throughout his tenure, for much of which I was chef de cabinet to the Director-General, Waldheim came frequently and treated me as part of his executive office. He liked to keep his European roots well mulched, and his daughter lived there. She was employed at the UN, in the division dealing with narcotic drugs. She was already a UN staff member at the time of her father's election. When it was diplomatically hinted to escape the charge of nepotism that she move sideways, to EFTA, the European Free Trade Association headquartered in Geneva, or to the Austrian diplomatic service, she remonstrated, insisting that she had been employed by the UN before him. She was her father's daughter. I came to know her quite well.

And Waldheim I was beginning to know – his instinctive reactions, his priorities, his approach to problems – when he sprang a surprise. He was walking through the Palais accompanied by the Director-General, his preferred security officer to one side, others trailing behind when the security officer, Don Thomas, dropped back to say the Secretary-General wished to speak to me personally – on a confidential matter. Waldheim took me aside, away from Winspeare, who, I was sure, disapproved of such hierarchical incorrectness, said he had something to ask me. Would I come for a drink that evening at the apartment of Liselotte, his daughter? Of course, I said. Around six-thirty I presented myself without any idea what the invitation entailed.

It was not a party. I was introduced to Woody Allen, or so I thought until he told me his name was Natural. I was handed a drink, just, and asked to sit, then Waldheim spoke. He would like me to help with the arrangements for Liselotte's wedding; she was to be married to the young man called Natural, in Geneva. They would like my assistance with practical matters. Ordering champagne was one. When I asked how much, he said that Liselotte would confirm the number of guests being invited. At three to the bottle? I said, remembering vaguely that from Oxford as normal reception consumption.

No, no, that was too much, Waldheim remonstrated making me feel a boozer, a quarter bottle per head was sufficient. He emphasised that full advantage should be taken of his diplomatic privileges. I was told to keep meticulous accounts of every single item of expenditure because the bridegroom's father, in keeping with Swiss custom, wished to pay half the cost.

When the great day arrived I felt as responsible for the weather as for everything else. Thank goodness it did not rain, which would have been attributed to my inattention if not incompetence. The small village church was charming. Liselotte was beautifully dressed. Her father smiled as benignly as Waldheim could in giving his daughter in marriage to someone he surely considered unworthy. The reception passed without incident only because I had cautioned the restaurant to have several cases of champagne in reserve – to be reimbursed at duty-free prices. That kept the champagne flowing, at roughly three guests to the bottle, until the family went for their grand wedding breakfast.

On Waldheim's next visit he called for the accounts. Everything, every stamp, every minor incidental expense, was to be listed and divided, precisely, between him and the bridegroom's father. He checked the arithmetic and signed me off duty. A week or two later he was back and the security officer appeared in my office with a large, very large, rectangular parcel. Before the brown paper wrapping came off I guessed the content. It was a huge enlargement of Waldheim's official photograph in full colour, ordinarily framed. An impressive gesture, certainly, but not easy to place. Nor was it personal. At least it needed his signature, preferably a dedication. I summoned up courage to thank Waldheim for his picture, much appreciated, but would he be so kind as to sign it, I asked. In came the picture, at which Waldheim exclaimed: 'But zat is not for you. Zat is for Liselott.' I wondered what she would do with it. Instead I received a smallish black and white print. That he duly signed before reverting to his political default mode.

The Security Council again addressed the latest major crisis in the run-up to Christmas 1975 and decided on action just before the holidays. To general consternation the Portuguese had abandoned their colony of East Timor leaving Indonesian forces to invade. But Indonesia was an influential third world country, oil producing, friend of America, pro-western though also on good terms with Soviet Russia. That it was also geographically strategic came into the equation. That and staunch support given by China in the Council to the anti-Indonesian movement. The Security Council was stymied, uncertain how to act. President Ford and Henry Kissinger had been in Jakarta on the eve of the Indonesian invasion thus seeming to condone it, as action intended to prevent the spread of communism. In the Council the United States preferred doing absolutely nothing, a policy proudly implemented by Ambassador Moynihan. Human rights groups made that difficult, not least in Australia where these were outspoken and loud, although the Australian government was reluctant to offend its populous northern neighbour. Not for the first time the Council stalled, deciding to have the Secretary-General send a mission and report in the New Year, in 1976.

I was away on holiday when the call came with instructions to join Winspeare, who had been named the Secretary-General's representative, as his deputy. Being on leave away from my office, I had neither administrative support nor briefing. East Timor was in the press, but press reports in my experience were rarely balanced or complete though some facts were clear. When Portugal imploded at home after the fall of Salazar, its overseas possessions, especially the most remote and least valuable, were left hanging in the air – if Timor, last major island in the Indonesian archipelago, can be said to hang in the air.

East Timor had been Portuguese for centuries. It became Portuguese in the great days of Portugal's maritime empire; a statue of Prince Henry the Navigator peering out to sea dominated the approach to Dili, the capital. From a coaling station, where ships took on water and fresh food, the colony developed with the export of camphor. In the tropics especially, camphor was precious. It protected clothes, preserving them and much else from the depredations of termites, ants and other insects. For centuries camphor-wood lined chests were standard equipment among Europeans in the East. East Timor benefited. In modern times, as the market for camphor declined, East Timor was left with little to sell overseas. Unimportant and remote as it was, it imported: it became a depository for political undesirables, those opposing fascist dictatorship, who were exiled by the Salazar regime. But that was not its only non-commercial value. Eastern Timor commanded straits of special importance to shipping, in particular the deep water channel from the South China Sea and the Pacific to the seas surrounding Australia, which permitted the submerged passage of nuclear submarines.

Abrupt regime change in Portugal left Timor's colonial administrators uncertain how to act, how to report and to whom, and profoundly nervous about their personal future. The native Timorese sensed opportunity. Though less than a dozen locals had higher education, of those four were priests, there was an exceptional degree of political awareness. Of Salazar's political exiles some had married local women, settled and fathered politically conscious sons. Not surprisingly, most were left wing. They formed the Fretelin party, modelled on similar movements in other Portuguese colonies, to campaign for independence. These were cold war days and Fretelin looked east not west. In addition to a dynamic leadership the party benefited from a degree of competent organisation that permitted it to seize a major arms depot left behind by Portuguese officials when they abandoned the mainland for the relative safety of Atauro, an off-shore island. Indonesia chose that moment to invade. President Suharto and the Indonesian military refused to countenance an independent entity, with communist sympathies, at the tip of their archipelago, and potentially strategic.

Indonesian troops marched into East Timor from the western half of the island, once Dutch controlled and already part of Indonesia. The invasion, they claimed in justification, was their response to an appeal for help from Fretelin's adversary, the Apodeti party. Indonesian numbers, weaponry and support systems gave them overwhelming advantage and despite fierce resistance Indonesia was able to entrench itself in Dili, at the airport in Bacau and to establish a foothold in two other towns. Fretelin supporters withdrew to the mountainous interior, beyond Indonesian reach, and to waging diplomatic war from Australia and elsewhere. They were lucky in having the energetic Jose Ramos-Horta, whose line of descent was similar to other leaders. Years later he shared the Nobel Prize, but that must have been a very unlikely prospect at the time. He proved an effective advocate in mobilising international awareness and support.

It took decades, and might never have succeeded but for the ending of the cold war, and Indonesia's own economic crisis and radical change in domestic politics. In 1976 neither seemed remotely likely. As an oil producer Indonesia had influential friends, principally the US, but not only. The Soviet Union saw no merit in criticizing Indonesia, and Britain looked to official Australian interests, principally the preference of a thinly populated continent, not to risk antagonising a close neighbour overflowing with people. Only China, in the Security Council, reproached Indonesia, called for invading forces to be withdrawn, and expressed support for Fretelin. China's diplomatic stance mattered, but weaponery mattered more.

Having lived in south-east Asia I remembered hearing that during the second world war Australian troops had tied down vastly superior Japanese forces in the Timorese interior. The Aussies could not defeat the Japs; they could make their campaign disproportionately costly. The near inaccessible, broken terrain, suited guerrilla fighting perfectly. All that guerrillas needed was for supplies to be air-dropped and ammunition. Was it conceivable that China would do that for Fretelin fighters? The Indonesian army was less resilient than the Japanese and less disciplined. Under sustained pressure it might falter. Winspeare and I met with a Chinese deputy minister. Any interview conducted through interpreters is never easy but Winspeare was able to formulate a question to the minister, designed, diplomatically, to explore how far, in practical and other ways, Chinese support for Fretelin might go. Following interpretation there was pause. The minister said something to his interpreter before answering. As translated he stated simply 'Indonesia will break up anyway.' A dramatic assertion.

There was no obvious way to decipher the implications of this cryptic statement. Winspeare smiled politely, he wondered when the minister thought that would happen. The minister continued to look inscrutable. We did not really expect a reply. Then he said: 'Within the next hundred years.' From that I drew two conclusions. First, that there would be no material Chinese challenge to Indonesia's occupation of Timor. Second, I saw the enormous political advantage the Chinese have in international negotiation. They are the only major country that can afford a truly long-term view. Western society lacks the patience, it craves results, and soon. In democratic states the government in power needs success during its term of office, before the next election.

As part of my briefing no mention had been made of the US position. Until I read his memoirs *A Dangerous Place,* I had no idea how determined Moynihan, as American ambassador to the UN following instructions from Washington, was that nothing happen. The speed, or rather lack of speed, with which the Council had acted, the wording of the mandating resolution, the relaxed deployment of our mission, implied no urgency. But differences within the Council often accounted for delay. The aggressor, in this case, was Indonesia, influential third world country, oil rich, strategically sited, on excellent relations with the US and on good enough terms with most other major powers. Indonesia had previously been authorised to swallow West Irian simply because it had been a Dutch possession. Washington wanted inaction. Moynihan achieved total success. I never heard of how much real politik Winspeare was informed when summoned to meet Waldheim in person.

In Dili we encountered stage-managed support for Indonesia. A meeting with the Timorese bishop was blocked 'for security reasons'. Dom Martinho da Costa Lopes was the apostolic administrator, not strictly speaking bishop, who showed rare courage in accusing Indonesia of atrocities. A letter of his was to lead to debate in the Australian parliament and Martinho was reassigned by a Vatican hierarchy concerned for Roman Catholics in Indonesia. He was replaced by Carlos Ximenes Belo, who emerged as equally courageous but was able to navigate as a remarkable leader of his people while ensuring that Indonesia did not oust him. Dom Martinho, had we met him, would undoubtedly have influenced what would have to be reported to New York. In response to efforts to reach the Fretelin leadership messages were received proposing a meeting on the south coast of the island where the Indonesians were not in full control; the Portuguese navy had promised to make available a corvette. I urged Winspeare that we should try despite the straits shark-infested reputation, but he refused.

Winspeare with his team in Dili, EastTimor

Years later when I had sight of confidential archives I discovered that the Indonesian armed forces, including naval, had orders to prevent our mission landing, making the venture hazardous in the extreme. Waldheim, knowing the US position, may well have instructed Winspeare to be circumspect, cautious rather than taking any unnecessary risk that Indonesia might consider provocative. I was never told. But that could account for failure to insist on meeting the bishop and abandoning our crossing of the Timor Sea. Subsequent lethargic Council consideration of the mission report, which I had conscientiously drafted, showed the remarkable lack of urgency on the Council's part and how little the Security Council seemed to care.

From Timor's political disaster we returned to disaster in Geneva. In

Winspeare's absence the director of administration, head of personnel and others concerned had approved a routine survey. In fact, not quite routine. The pay scale for Geneva general service salaries was set by comparison with local wages, unlike professional staff whose salaries were standardised internationally with a cost of living allowance according to post. Comparable local salaries were never easy to establish. A senior secretary in a Swiss private bank, for example, was exceedingly well compensated to ensure secrecy for numbered accounts. No UN secretary had access to information that valuable. The administration traditionally sought sensible compromise through talks with staff representatives. When the staff council urged an up-dated survey of Geneva wages the administration used financial stringency to refuse. The staff council insisted.

Discreet soundings suggested that UN pay scales were not disadvantageous; it might be best to leave well alone, and save the expense of a costly survey. The staff council still insisted. The administration capitulated but thought of a ruse: if comparable local salaries proved lower, UN pay scales would have to be reduced. The survey took place. Local salaries were marginally higher. The staff council rejoiced, and demanded immediate upward adjustment for general service personnel. The administration, with the UN lacking adequate resources, was unable to deliver. The council called for a strike, without precedent, and hugely detrimental to the UN image at a time of severe budgetary restraint when Geneva staff were widely perceived as living well. People were outraged. *Time* magazine carried to the world a severely critical article entitled 'The Good Life by the Lake'.

Winspeare and I returned to a Palais without heat – it was February – without light, and without power most of the time, which disabled electric typewriters, and bitter confrontation. Administrators found staff representatives quite unreasonable; the staff representatives rejected any dealing with administrators who had tried to trick them. Winspeare was suddenly held responsible for a tense and disagreeable situation not of his making. His strength was diplomacy not personnel management. Encounters with excited representatives consumed enormous time and energy, almost as much as trying to pacify headquarters in New York, where the Palais was accused of administrative incompetence. The Timor report, which we would normally have discussed in minute detail, was left to me. My secretary took drafts home to type. Only when I came into my office at the weekend did I find it warm with power restored; the strike leaders included technicians who knew that the huge windows in the new extension would crack if a certain temperature were not maintained, and they might be held responsible.

When Waldheim visited Geneva shortly afterwards, on this occasion with his wife, Mr and Mrs Winspeare gave a dinner. They invited me; it was to be an opportunity for me to brief the Secretary-General informally about Timor and discover how he wished to proceed. Waldheim was not greatly interested. He cornered Winspeare about the strike. That he wanted to talk about: steps to be taken against those with administrative responsibility for having provoked the strikers. Three principals were to be removed from their posts and reassigned, not sacked or formally demoted but transferred to much less desirable positions. Winspeare's deputy as director-general, in theoretical charge during our absence on mission, was elderly and approaching retirement age; there could be no question of extending his contract. The Secretary-General announced that he had decided on a comprehensive administrative review of the Geneva office.

The humiliation of being subjected to review did nothing for Winspeare's morale. As a man of honour he accepted responsibility, at his level, for a situation that was unlikely to have arisen had he not been on mission. Nor did it improve his relationship with Waldheim, which had never been easy. The antipathy, I imagine, was mutual. Winspeare as a young Italian foreign service officer untainted by Fascism – he had been of the king's party – was entrusted after the second world war with reopening their embassy in London. There he met his Austrian-born wife who had driven ambulances in England when her family left Vienna in revulsion at the Anschluss, Austria's incorporation into Nazi Germany. Waldheim's war had been in collaboration with the Germans; his father having changed the family name from Vaclavik. The Winspeare Guicciardis were an old aristocratic family, though Winspeare was not at all snobbish.

To those who did not know him well he could seem aloof, or humourless. Not the case. It helped to understand his anglophile old school values and sense of humour. I remember his meeting the Polish ambassador in the Palais corridor. Wyzner, tall, spoke excellent English and French, and was the most engaging of ambassadors from communist eastern Europe, and the only one to wear suits that fitted. On that occasion he was in brown. 'Surely a gentleman only wears brown when it's tweed,' Winspeare said smiling. Wyzner smiled back though I doubt he had a clue what that quaint English mannerism was about. Eugenie Wyzner had a knack of smiling through. Brown-suited or not he survived as a latter day Vicar of Bray. After Geneva, back at the ministry in Warsaw, I encountered him when on an official visit. At luncheon he was charming, friendly, shrugged a shoulder and smiled wanly when I nodded at his 'Comrade Wyzner' place-card. Later he was appointed Polish ambassador to the UN in New York and, when Poland changed regime moved to a senior secretariat position. His career culminated as ambassador once more representing post-communist independent Poland.

For me working closely with Winspeare in Geneva as well as on mission was always instructive and usually pleasant. Invariably the consummate diplomat; I realised later how much of my own behaviour I was to model on his. A congenial travelling companion too, when you shared his sense of humour, and at table together always willing to recount personal anecdotes. Committed though he was to the United Nations, Winspeare never achieved UN insidership. He was Geneva-based, not at New York headquarters where personal relations easily developed and wheeler-dealing took place. Second, his apparent detachment, the old fashioned manner, was out of synchronisation with the nineteen-seventies post-colonial world. The Tunisian head of personnel was quoted as disparaging *'le petit aristocracie du Palais'* – Winspeare was a baron, and the chief of protocol, a Belgian count. Winspeare considered demeaning the give and take of career bartering, not only as undignified but inappropriate to international service. Maurice Strong, a rising environment star with contemporary north American business style, outraged Winspeare by proposing a 'deal'. Winspeare reacted strongly, as if to a threat, provoking the retort: 'I am better as a friend than enemy.' They were not friends from then on. Nor did Winspeare win friends by being rule-bound when requested to authorise official cars for visiting officials from New York.

Bahrain had been a triumph and Winspeare treasured the UN peace medal awarded him by U Thant. The India, Pakistan and Bangladesh mission had been interesting, important and worthwhile. East Timor less so, sensitive and complex though it was. That was to be his last mission as relations with Waldheim, never cordial, deteriorated further. Winspeare was too consistent, committed to the values he inherited, from his upbringing and the war years, for personal compromise. He did not deserve to end his career at the UN as he did.

He retired to live quietly in Geneva, to some extent a disappointed man, and without securing positions for his immediate office, as if he had lost faith. I had not seen him for months when he appeared one day on his way to the post office in the Palais. He was well, he said, and asked after my family. 'I haven't noticed you here before,' I said, which made him laugh. 'Do you know that for over forty years I never once set foot in a post office, there was always someone to handle letters. Actually, I am enjoying it.'

15 Another Italian Dirgen

His SUCCESSOR, from 1977, another Italian diplomat, had three things in common with Winspeare. He was Italian, unusually tall for an Italian, and married to an Austrian. In every other respect they could not have been less alike. Luigi Cottafavi was sociable, not very profound, with a relaxed approach to office discipline. Personably likeable, and he liked people. He was quick to say that he wished me to continue as his Chef de Cabinet, that as a newcomer to the UN he counted on me. I was relieved; it scotched the anxiety stimulated by an Italian colleague who had telephoned from Rome to assure me, sweetly, that they would find me an agreeable alternative position when he became Chef de Cabinet as Gigi wanted – calling Cottafavi Gigi to prove intimacy.

Unveiling by Lady Soames in the presence of Luigi Cottafavi of my friend Edwina Sandys' sculpture 'Family' in the Palais grounds, Geneva

Gigi, as I also came to call him after retirement, was easy to work with, liked to be known as 'Deargen' his take on 'Dirgen' the official designation in cables. He habitually delegated substantive matters, which suited me. He also delegated tiresome visitors, self-important persons who insisted on meeting the Director-General and whose business might be embarrassing. A telegram from New York addressed to Cottafavi confirmed the imminent arrival of an ambassador from a small country. The ambassador claimed close friendship with Waldheim, they had earlier been accredited in the same capital, and the Secretary-General had assured him that a suitable assignment could be found at the Geneva office now that he wished to be based in Europe. Cottafavi, concerned for his own contractual status, was reluctant to risk offending Waldheim. The ambassador was likely to be arrogant and demanding, and Cottafavi knew we had no highish level vacancy to propose. That lovely day in early May Gigi absented himself from the office on urgent unexpected business deputing me to receive the ambassador.

He was predictably arrogant, displeased to have the Director-General unavailable. He was indeed, he insisted, a good friend of Waldheim, as we must have heard from New York; his wife, incidentally, was Austrian and knew Mrs Waldheim well. I had presumably been informed that he was assured of a suitable appointment in Geneva. My only recourse was flattery. As an ambassador he rightly aspired to a full directorship. 'Absolutely,' he said. In the office there were four of that rank, all currently filled with no incumbent about to depart, I told him. But he might be willing to consider deputy director. He nodded. I went through with him every post at that level in the UN Geneva. All were filled, though one retirement was due in nine months time. That was not good enough, he interrupted before I could even mention a possibility of the retiree being extended. He had to have something by September when his children started school. I did not imagine, I said, that as a senior ambassador he would be interested in anything at a lesser level. He blustered, said he was extremely disappointed in how he had been treated, was sure the Secretary-General would insist. Having done his utmost to embarrass me, he left.

Cottafavi sneaked back for a full account and to watch me prepare a cable for the SG's office. It was a good thing I had a permanent contract, he wished to reassure me. But no explosion followed, no irate, even critical response. It transpired that the man had been badgering Waldheim for a job. The wife was Austrian, it was true, and they had once been accredited in the same capital, but Waldheim admitted to knowing him only superficially and saw no political advantage in helping him secure a UN appointment. Somebody else though had to say 'no'.

Access to the Director-General's office was restricted to persons with convincing reason to go above division heads. In practice we received anyone steadfastly refusing to be directed elsewhere or sufficiently insistent. Problems were rare. When security called it was usually possible to suggest how to handle querulous visitors. One morning security called, then called again to say that a youngish woman was adamant in wanting to see the Director-General. She refused to state her business. When told that the Director-General was occupied, she reacted hysterically. Nor would she go away. Cottafavi suggested I see her. In walked a woman, in her early twenties, clearly distraught. She was stateless, she blurted out, had no country, nowhere to live, and it was all the UN's fault. She was nothing if not articulate; words flowed in an uninterrupted stream, and gradually the story surfaced. It began with her mother.

The mother was Russian, well educated, a linguist, who worked as a translator. During the war she met, fell in love with and married a Pole, who happened to be Jewish. She became pregnant and had a child. In the immediate post-war confusion the couple became separated and lost track of each other. With her daughter the mother lived in Moscow where as a respected translator she enjoyed commensurate privileges, not least her extensive library of valuable books. Years later, years throughout which there had been no communication, a letter arrived. The Pole wrote to say that he had emigrated to Israel where he now lived. He thought constantly of the woman he had married and all he wanted was to be reunited with her and their daughter. The mother was deeply moved. She had never forgotten falling in love. But emigration to Israel from the Soviet Union was anything but easy. It was dangerous even to apply. Once you applied you were outcast without even the assurance of being granted an exit visa in due course. She said she would come. She lost employment as a translator. And to pay for permission and the expenses involved sold all her precious books. Eventually, mother and daughter were authorised to travel knowing they would forfeit Soviet citizenship and the right ever to return.

Not surprisingly, after so long apart, life in the reunited family failed to meet expectations. They struggled together. The daughter was admitted to an Israeli school. Then the parents divorced. All very sad but I must admit to finding it hard to grasp how the UN was to blame. The divorce did it. Indirectly. While the father was Jewish and fully integrated in Israeli society, the mother was not, nor was the daughter. Jewishness passes by descent through the mother, not the father. Mother and daughter, not being Jews, began finding life difficult. The mother, disillusioned, wrote to her sister in Moscow that living in Israel was very different to what she had imagined, leaving much to be desired. That letter, intercepted by Soviet censors, was to be quoted freely by Soviet delegates in UN human rights debate. Israeli authorities took virulent exception. They made life virtually impossible for mother and daughter. The mother encountered immense difficulty in obtaining employment and the daughter, so she said, was obliged to leave her Israeli school. The mother might, just might, have been able to crawl humiliated back to Russia, but not the daughter.

Since this was all the UN's fault, it was for the UN to help, she insisted emotionally. Although in no real sense was it UN responsibility, the suffering was real. Two human beings had become snared in the absurd injustices of our world. The girl was stateless but she did not qualify as a refugee. No country felt any obligation to accept her. We took the case up formally with the Swiss authorities and I was relieved when after consideration Switzerland agreed to grant both the daughter and her mother political asylum.

Diplomatic life also had its pleasant side. I enjoyed receptions and especially the dinner parties at which business was handled discreetly in congenial surroundings. Unlike UN staff who did not have official housing most member states heads of mission lived in desirable properties beautifully sited near the lake of Geneva. There they were expected to offer hospitality as an essential part of their assignment. Personal relations could be valuable in resolving problems, generating trust, and creating opportunities to touch on semi-confidential aspects or information not included in official correspondence. I remember numerous issues, such as the non-Jewish ex-Russian, that were helpfully first broached in an informal setting. Very occasionally, something altogether unexpected arose to divert proceedings. The New Zealand ambassador was giving a pleasant dinner party at which I found myself seated beside the wife of the Syrian ambassador, an elegant Arabic woman who to my surprise spoke excellent English. We had not met before but conversation flowed easily when it emerged that she had been at Oxford and had thoroughly enjoyed it. We talked of mundane matters, no politics, so readily that I neglected any social duty to alternate conversation with the person on my other side. Pudding having been served the ambassador clinked his champagne glass, he wished to propose a toast. We waited. 'To President Sadat' he said. The Syrian ambassador's wife erupted, this elegant, civilized woman came close to screaming: Sadat deserved not honour but desecration, he had sold the Palestinians down the river. The Camp David accords were a scandal. She, though she did not say so, was Palestinian.

Kurt Waldheim holding a press conference in Geneva.
Luigi Cottafavi and Erik Jensen are seated behind

In UN circles Camp David was interpreted by most as a positive achievement, though Waldheim resented having been eclipsed. He was increasingly obsessed by his image internationally. By his second term I had come to know Waldheim well enough and his political priorities and he knew me. I continued to function intermittently as special assistant when he came to Geneva without his personal staff. When my name was proposed in 1979 for a senior post in New York Waldheim summoned me to the hotel room he used as an office. He supported my candidature, he said, but there were certain constraints. He then outlined the characteristics of the strongest candidates for available directorships. He needed to satisfy the aspirations of certain relevant member states, more specifically states he had recently visited and some he would be visiting. It sounded Habsburgian. Mine was the only instance where he emphasised the qualifications required for a particular post – arguably because it was the only one directly implicating the thirty-eighth floor, his executive office.

16 Special political questions: African crises

I WAS ONLY FORTY-SIX when I became the director in the office for Special Political Questions in the Secretary-General's executive office. That was a source of some personal satisfaction. Abdulrahim Abby Farah, former Somali ambassador and representative on the Security Council, was the Under-Secretary-General. While it was not explicit in the title, ours was the Secretary-General's office dealing with the African continent, apart from the middle east. Abby Farah made himself Africa's spokesman in the secretariat, and Africa in the eighties needed all possible advocacy and aid. Abby had expected to appoint as director an African. But he was reluctant to have his choice offend the other African ambassadors who were lobbying intensively for the post. Finally, it was Waldheim himself who insisted on an appointment, and named me. His patience had been stretched by demands constantly arising from a continent in disarray and criticism of his apparent lack of concern. Countries traumatised by civil war, revolution, violent regime change, the overthrowing of despots or widespread misgovernment appealed for assistance to the international community. As in Biafra they needed aid fully as much as those afflicted by natural disaster. This I came to see for myself, travelling to obscure places, to states few people had heard of, beginning in 1980 with Chad.

Chad to an American is a hanging bit of punched voting slip made infamous by the contested Florida recount that bought George W. Bush the presidency. Chad to older Britons is a cartoon head peering above a wall. Chad is also a country. A vast expanse of land dividing Nigeria from the Sudan, the northern half is desert, populated sparsely by semi-nomadic Arabic-speaking and Islamic tribes, the southern region is sub-tropical with people who were animists, some becoming Christian, and who practice agriculture. It is, of course, a colonial construct, offspring of French Equatorial Africa. Civil war between north and south would have seemed logical, but Chad's history of civil warfare has revolved more round rival northern factions. One or other party looked sometimes to France, occasionally to Libya, for material support.

Between them they destroyed such infrastructure as existed and the once charmingly avenued capital of Ndjamena, whose maiden name had been Fort Lamy.

Hissene Habre, head of one faction, despite ties to France had made himself internationally unpopular by holding hostage a group of French nationals in the 1970s. He was made Prime Minister of Chad in 1978, but ousted by Goukouni Ouedeye, who replaced French elements with Libyan, including troops. Goukouni had Chad appeal to the international community for special economic assistance. The airport near Ndjamena remained out of bounds, Libyan-controlled, as well as shell damaged. Access lay through Cameroon, the last, long miles by rough track, bumped in a Land Rover, to the banks of the Shari. No serviceable bridge survived. Small, hand-paddled dug-outs took us across, manoeuvring cautiously between a multitude of semi-submerged hippopotami in the river. They looked harmless. But we were sternly advised to leave them well alone. Our boatman watched for any movement as he paddled circumspectly, alert for any sudden stirring that might overturn the boat. Docile, vegetarian, though it is, the hippopotamus is a large, large animal, which counts on being treated with respect and every hippopotamus mother is fiercely protective of her young. All continued munching peacefully as we crossed before stumbling ashore on the far bank.

With grounds running down to the Chari river, La Tchadienne, in peace-time, had been an attractive hotel. Fighting changed that. Little furniture remained in the rooms, and that was mostly broken. Water ceased to run into the filth encrusted basin; half a bucketful was issued us each day, for all purposes. The door to my room, on the ground floor, flimsily constructed from a single sheet of hardboard, was perforated with bullet holes. We were given little or nothing to eat; fortunately I had my habitual travelling reserve stock of raisins. The country's dilemma was everywhere to be seen. Goukouni's people bolstered their case with extreme visual aids. They insisted that I visit a gigantic warehouse. It served as depository for skulls, piled high, and jumbled bones, all attributed to the atrocities of the other side. In its crudity, the lack of any organisation, even any simulated respect for the dead, the mortuary resembled the haunted house from a fun-fair side-show – except it was real.

The airport, less ghoulish, was another obligatory exhibit. The airport itself was occupied by Libyan troops and out of bounds to Chadians and others. I was urged to see for myself the problems this generated, not by attempting to penetrate the airport confines, but by driving along a nearby road. An armed escort would be provided. The armed escort turned out to be a single Chadian soldier slumped over his weapon in the front seat, next the driver. The driver, we were told, carried an official laissez-passer issued by the government ensuring our safe conduct. Three of us, the UNICEF and WFP representatives and myself, were squeezed into the car's backseat. The exercise had little point, beyond enabling us to confirm, from personal observation, the difficulties arising from foreign occupation of the airport. We were driving cautiously, but not too slowly, past a check-point, when a Libyan soldier emerged. The driver waved our *laissez-passer,* displaying it open. To no effect. The Libyan soldier advanced, cocking his rifle. The driver stopped dead. Our escort came to with a start, but fumbling with his gun let it slip through his legs as the Libyan threw open the door. Very aggressively the Libyan spat: 'Francais?' Our UNICEF friend thought he meant French-speaking and was mouthing 'oui' when the WFP representative, himself an Italian, grasped the situation; he almost shouted, loudly, emphatically: 'Non, no. Italiano.' At which the Libyan broke into a huge smile and waved us through. Colonial history has strange consequences.

Efforts to mobilise aid for Goukouni were disrupted when he was overthrown by his predecessor Hissene Habre. A second mission to Chad in 1981 followed. I suspect it was exactly the same grim mortuary exhibit, now attributed to Goukouni's people, that Hissene Habre's supporters brought us to marvel at when we returned to Ndjamena. There were a few changes for the better: limited airport access, some reconstruction, a functioning restaurant or two, and, I was told, a night club. The new foreign minister, Miskine, was the first Chadian whom I found direct, apparently honest and open to advice. We worked constructively together on an assistance package for presentation to a donor conference that I was asked to organise. The conference achieved respectable pledges. Unfortunately, renewed unrest in Chad impeded making the help as effective as it could have been. Political in-fighting never ceased. I heard that Miskine, young, tough and very fit, had died – of malaria, they said.

If I had been only marginally aware of Chad before going there, I think I knew little more about the Comoros, Les Isles Comores. New York issued me tickets to Dar-es-Salaam with a confirmed onward connecting flight. It was a good connection, according to the travel agency, no need even for a night's stop-over. The UNDP resident representative had therefore been alerted but not asked for special support. It was a very long journey from New York to Dar. I stumbled from the aircraft, as one does after endless hours flying across time zones, only to be told there was no connecting flight. 'Tomorrow,' said someone in uniform. To my relief the resident representative had sent a man to the airport. Of course, he knew nothing about flights, but he had a car. He took me to Dar's modern-style hotel. I was shown to a room, on the first floor, with a view into banana fronds. This was all that was pretty about it. The hotel had been built for air-conditioning, and the air-conditioning did not work. Generated electricity produced only enough for a feeble glow in one solitary light-bulb. To see in the bathroom the same bulb had to accompany me. The single towel was a rag any housewife would have rejected as a dish-cloth. The room was thick with heat. I slid open a window, which jammed and would not close before mosquitoes surged through into every corner, nook and cranny. I passed a night best not to remember.

Next morning the resident representative came to apologise. Not his fault, of course, but he was accustomed to apologising to officials transiting Dar. There would be no flight to Comoros that day he told me when I said that I expected to be off in a matter of hours. Nor, when I checked, was one scheduled for the day following. A clerk suggested brightly that I rent a car and drive to Nairobi – he was confident that my lack of visa would be waived – where there might be an earlier connection to Moroni, capital of Grand Comore. Since no one was remotely sure I opted to stay in Tanzania the extra day or two, but out of town. Just north of Dar was a 'beach resort' with a tourist hotel. It was empty. Once again a single bulb served bedroom and bathroom. But the hotel did overlook the Indian Ocean, although I could not see as far as the Comoros islands, and some of the time they had beer.

With their Comoros colony the French had been crafty. To maintain a foothold in the waters off East Africa they offered independence isle by isle. The result: Mayotte voted to remain an overseas province of metropolitan France, with significant schooling and health benefits compensating for loss of national pride, while the rest of the archipelago, led by the main island of Grand Comore, became independent and was launched on an African trajectory of instability, multiple coups d'etat, and an unreliable economy. Prolonged political unrest deterred investment and undermined most efforts at economic development. The country appealed to the UN for special economic assistance and that was why I had come.

Landing at dusk we confronted the Comoros' surviving and most assertive crop. Ylang-ylang grows profusely and especially at evening exudes an overwhelming scent. Diluted and refined, like a cocktail spirit, it makes a base for more sophisticated perfumery. Over time it had served the economy well, but it was not sufficient. The Comoros were unable to compete in world vanilla and pepper markets. The other projected earner, tourism, had yet to happen. One problem, apart from being sunny in a region of sunshine, was the lack of beaches. There was one, with black volcanic sand. The singular, unique tourist attraction, the coelocanth, deep sea prehistoric survivor from early evolution, was not often to be seen, if at all, except in the name of a fish restaurant.

With compact space and few diversions the mission completed its work in a couple of days. Top of the government's wish list was a plane to be provided by the international community. My advisors, without exception, ruled against it. Not remotely justified by the number of projected passengers, they argued, and the islands lacked maintenance capacity, barely coping with the needs of the one aircraft they already had. If, on occasion, a replacement was required, it made infinitely better sense to rent one. A list of more sensible assistance needs followed. It was for me, at the concluding meeting with the President, to persuade him that Comorian interests would be better served by giving priority to the most convincing items. Putting an aircraft first would jeopardise the seriousness of our aid plan. Principal donors had their own sources, well-informed, to give advice. The President did not take kindly to my counsel.

He received me in the presidential villa, rather ordinary ex-colonial quarters. The reception room was of modest middle-class dimensions, blacked out against the sunlight and jerkily air-conditioned. The furniture consisted of a desk at one end, an impressively large desk, and at the other end a sofa, two upright chairs and a low table. I was ushered to the far end. The President, from his ornately carved throne-chair behind the desk, invited me to be seated. He hoped that I was having an enjoyable visit to the Comoros, beautiful islands with great tourist potential. He cleared his throat, the tone of his voice changed and he launched into a speech.

Like Gladstone, like Bhutto, he addressed me loudly, enunciating forcefully, as if I were the town meeting, his oratory rolling about in the confined space. He seemed to look through me, or over me, to a wider audience. For nearly half an hour this continued. Bombastic, meandering and diffuse, it defied summary. But a leitmotif emerged. The President referred time and again to an aircraft, the vital importance of an additional plane for Comoros stability and economic development. I understand why he was assassinated later – though that may be unfair. He struck me as pathetic, rather than pompous, self-important and determined to assert his importance, perhaps knowing his real power to be marginal.

After twenty-five minutes he stopped speaking. Acclamation, not comment, was called for. I paid tribute, a mild compliment or two, appreciation for the courtesy shown my mission and his personal openness in elaborating on their needs. The aircraft was undoubtedly important, I conceded, but we had to prepare the ground with donors. The best way forward might be to present some preliminary needs, leading up to a plane. I worked pedantically through this seam, using varied language to rehearse the same argument, and continued talking in a monotonous tone gradually winding down like an old-fashioned gramophone. As if reluctantly convinced and without further comment, he stopped listening. The audience had ended.

On my way out the President shook my hand and asked: '*Est ce que vous êtes marié, Monsieur?*' I said I was.

'*J'ai un petit cadeau pour votre dame. Et pour vous, Monsieur.*'

At that moment I visualised some precious looking object that I would be obliged to decline, which was bound to give offence.

He summoned an Aide, who primly produced a small tin box.

'*C'est vanille, pour Madame.*'

He then presented me with another metallic container. It rattled. It was filled with pepper corns.

'*Ça vous donne de la force, Monsieur,*' said the President and with his left hand struck his right elbow making the forearm shoot up, fist clenched. He laughed.

I smiled gratefully, and saw no need to refuse.

We raised substantial aid, without an aircraft, which benefitted the country and the president before he was shot dead. In thirty years since becoming independent the Comoros experienced twenty coups d'état.

In 1981, 1982 and 1983 I also led missions to other African countries in great need: as well as the Comoros, Equatorial Guinea, Central African Republic, Djibouti and Guinea Bissau.

Among African states the Central African Republic had a reputation for misrule rather than coups d'état. As the Central African Empire it had been lorded over by the Emperor Bokassa. Bokassa had served in the French colonial forces, from corporal to officer, and admired French style – or his interpretation of it. France, under Giscard d'Estaing, wanting to secure its bases in that part of the continent, humoured Bokassa. When Bokassa, whose hero and ideal was Napoleon, planned an imperial coronation, he wished it modelled on that of Napoleon. He would crown himself at a magnificent ceremony in Bangui. His coronation carriage was to be drawn by the finest horses. France obligingly sent six superb Percheron, who all died in the blazing sun and equatorial heat of Bangui, but not before doing their duty.

Bokassa built himself a palace as for Africa's sun-king.

If Bangui was not quite Paris and the palace was no Versailles, it had an imposing entrance gateway and was surrounded by a park. The gateway proclaimed the emperor's glory. Carved on great columns were the numerous decorations with which he was honoured, achieved through comprehensive reciprocity between African leaders. Within the compound the 'deer park' had African animals. They performed less obligingly than deer but gratified the master. The lake was a pond, with crocodiles. Bokassa took pleasure in feeding his crocodiles – limbs of his adversaries.

The Emperor Bokassa knew himself out of the ordinary. His coronation announced it to the world; his palace confirmed it to whoever dared approach. He was a being above others. The law was his, to do with as he pleased. More than justice or others' pursuit of happiness his personal pleasure was what mattered to Bokassa. He enjoyed dancing and for himself and a French wife he had built an outdoor dance-floor in the open central courtyard of the palace. Set back a little to one side a neat row of maisonettes, like hotel 'family suites', accommodated other current favourites. Bokassa's appetite for women was famous; in Bangui it was inadvisable to look with the slightest hint of concupiscence on any young woman who might be appearing in the emperor's sights.

Inevitably, he overreached himself. It was written into the operatic scenario. Some dismembering of political opponents and feeding crocodiles with their remains could perhaps be expected, taking people's women was predictable, but Bokassa went too far, even for him. The fall from his pinnacle of grace was spectacular. He was brutally ousted in a military coup and thrown into prison. The miracle is that they did not tear him limb from limb or torture him to death. In the event he survived imprisonment and years later emerged to claim pension rights and a property in France. The officers who took power turned to the international community for help in recovering from imperially chaotic rule and national collapse. For a start they renamed the country the Central African Republic.

It was to the Central African Republic that I led a special economic assistance mission. I was first taken to see Bokassa's palace, no more flamboyantly occupied, and rapidly falling into disrepair. Animals once carolled in the 'deer park' had escaped back into the wild. The pond was emptied of crocodiles – with no one to feed them human titbits. The decoration embellished pillars remained at the entrance, like the pedestal in the sands round Ozymandias tumbled statue.

Returning from the palace we passed a roadside group. These are a common sight throughout much of Africa, commonly vendors with fruit for sale to passers-by. But these had nothing to sell. They stayed apart, looked away, as if by ignoring us they would be ignored. They were pygmies, who had ventured briefly out of their forest. The official accompanying us tried to pretend that no one had noticed them. Like things connected to Bokassa they belonged to an older, less modern past, of which the new regime wanted no reminding. The official never stopped talking of roads and bridges as we drove back into town and the aid they counted on receiving to help them, though not necessarily the pygmies, escape from what had been. The aid we mobilised might have achieved more had the officers who took control been motivated less by acquiring power than the prospect of improving conditions in their country.

Bangui sat beside the Congo. For me perhaps the most reassuring sight before leaving was to observe life on the great river. Men moved over the water in canoes too frail for purpose yet wonderfully adapted, struggled with vast nets, dispatched fish into baskets. Women worked along the banks. This was life as it had been for centuries, unaffected by Bokassa's coming and his passing, or any of the others moving in and out of the heart of darkness.

Djibouti had been the French territory of the Afars and Issas, an enclave artificially designated between Abyssinia and Somalia. For France it provided a base, and still did. But independence left the country dependent on a foreign presence and politically insecure. To bolster its confidence in feeling independent Djibouti asked the UN for special economic aid. Two memories of our mission stand out. The first, because UN personnel and I misjudged a need. Before departing New York I had been approached by a director of personnel and asked that I persuade the Djibouti government to present a qualified candidate for recruitment to the secretariat. Djibouti was one of only two or three member states unrepresented. I saw this as something of a gift.

Most third world countries clamoured for UN appointments; Djibouti could be expected to value this as a prize, a reward to be awarded someone favoured. I had never been comfortable with excessive emphasis on equitable geographical distribution, that UN mantra, which I thought prejudiced the highest standards of professional competence, but on that I was outnumbered. I did what had been officially requested. At a final audience with the President we reviewed the mission's conclusions, all very rational. I assured him of full support in impressing Djibouti's needs and aspirations on the General Assembly. He thanked me, graciously. Before rising to go, I mentioned our wish to have a Djibouti national recruited to the UN and assured him that a suitable vacancy would be found. I saw the anger rise in his face. The President, only moments before appreciative and friendly, snapped furiously. Djibouti had barely a handful of well-qualified people, university educated, and now we were trying to steal one away. That was the very last thing Djibouti needed to help it forward.

The second vivid memory is of being pressured to stay an additional day. The mission's work and the working week were done. Supplies were coming by train from Ethiopia, said the liaison officer discreetly, and the next day, a day of rest, would be spent chewing Qat. It was better than sex, he argued, but virtually a sexual experience. I was invited to remain as their official guest; it would be a pleasure for them and, he was sure, for me. Sometimes I wish I had.

There was nothing pleasurable about Equatorial Guinea. Another African state had been assembled out of disparate parts. The island of Fernando Po had been a Spanish colony; the name was familiar as the place where relief flights loaded and departed for Biafra; the capital Santa Isabel had meanwhile been renamed Malabo. Its people were mainly Bubis. The mainland opposite, Rio Muni, was populated by the Fang, and also belonged to Spain. At independence, the two were merged into one country. The populations competed for power.

The first head of the autonomous government was accused of plotting and executed by Macias Nguema, Fang of the Mongomo clan. As president for over a decade following Macias Nguema used the country for his personal advantage and that of his relatives. In the process they diverted what wealth the state possessed. From being a prosperous cocoa producer and exporter also of valuable timber, only one Spanish-run plantation survived. In 1979 Macias Nguema was liquidated following a palace coup and his nephew Obiang Nguema became president. Obiang Nguema gave even greater power to his Mongomo family. Human rights were totally ignored. If it were possible the situation in the country worsened.

When I visited in the early eighties the hotel room had nothing, and nothing worked. Brownish water trickled from a tap, without stopping. Electricity came occasionally and went. Food was almost non-existent. Incredible on an island surrounded by rich fishing, with a climate where bananas grow instinctively and chickens prosper on kitchen waste. But roving armed men made free with whatever they fancied. That was why fishermen ceased fishing. When you return not once, but twice or three times, with your catch, to have it looted at gunpoint, and consider yourself lucky to live, you leave the fishing-boat beached. For the same reason poultry vanished. It made no sense to nourish chickens for the next marauding band to steal.

Amid deprivation paraded one self-beacon of well-being: the United States embassy, shielded by security wire, defensive walling and patrolling guards, confident in its own secure communications, flew high the Stars and Stripes for all to admire. The American ambassador for a time was a hard right political appointee, Frank Ruddy, who was especially proud of his one achievement: Equatorial Guinea always voted 'with' the US in the UN General Assembly.

Equatorial Guinea had been reduced to requesting special economic assistance, and need it they did. Oil discoveries have since changed that; the scramble for wealth and unscrupulous foreign crooks are now the problem. Mark Thatcher and associates, with their bungled coup attempt, brought international awareness and implied that the country was a prize worth taking. At the time of my mission even special economic assistance made doubtful sense. Material aid was not what they needed. They needed responsible government, which was not forthcoming. So long as Bubis and Fang, and more especially clans within the Fang, battled brutally for power and the perks of power, there was little prospect of change. I argued forcefully with ministers that maintaining law and order and at least some respect for human rights, which I emphasised, would provide credibility to their campaign for international support. They listened, but showed little likelihood of adapting their priorities. Only when the peoples of Equatorial Guinea escaped from being hostage to tyrannizing dictatorship and achieved a degree of national reconciliation would they become able to realise the country's potential.

Conditions in Guinea Bissau were little better than in Equatorial Guinea. Bissau, however, had the merit of being home to a great resistance hero, Africa's answer to Che Guevara. Amilcar Lopes Cabral's portrait was everywhere. Like Che Guevara he was good-looking with a reputation for charisma. He was credited with leading his country to independence from Portugal and inspiring other leaders, who had become assimilated into metropolitan ways, to re-embrace African culture and create an independent African identity. Following an encouraging start, after Cabral's murder the country experienced more than one coup d'etat.

Bissau did not suffer from a tribal divide but it was neglected, lacked valuable natural resources and was incompetently governed. The population, extremely poor, had a life expectancy below the African average and substantially lower than world expectations. It needed help and seemed worth helping. Between ministerial meetings I was shown the countryside surrounding the principal town. There was little to impress, in nature or as made by man. Near the coast, starkly alone, stood a vast concrete structure. It could have been a prison, abandoned to tell from its state and the jungly growth proliferating around and on it. What was it? I asked. A fish-processing factory, the guide told me, donated by the Soviet Union. Then why wasn't it working? Because, he explained, the country had insufficient electricity to power the plant. No surprise, given the erratic supply to my hotel room. We were able to present to the General Assembly a seriously researched and convincingly worded appeal for aid, emphasising the challenges faced by Guinea-Bissau, its history and its legitimate aspirations.

All along the coast of West Africa lies a region of heat, heavy rainfall and luxuriant vegetation, where mosquitoes prosper and disease, gold attracting Arab and white traders, and the business of slavery. Slaves were traditionally widespread in the region - when later I first arrived in north-west Africa there were still recognized slaves in Mauritania. Powerful tribes made slaves of those weaker than themselves. Arabized peoples and Arabs inland undertook slaving expeditions for their own services and for sale. But the slavery market, as is all too well-known, swelled gruesomely when demand burgeoned in the Americas. Sugar, newly fashionable and lucrative, was labour-intensive, as was cotton.

Black slaves, manacled, chained in gangs, were marched to ports for transhipment. While waiting for a vessel they were packed into holding caverns near the coast. Some such caverns still exist. They are truly horrible when repopulated in the mind. The humiliation, pain, suffering and squalor are almost unimaginable; it is grotesque what human beings seem capable of doing to each other. I was taken to see an embarkation zone, an experience I shall not forget. After the legal abolition of slavery, first in the British Empire and later elsewhere, thousands of freed Africans returned from the Americas, north and south, to found Sierra Leone – Freetown – and Liberia and to reintegrate and reinhabit the world where their forebears had been born. Slavery, it strikes me, despite the caverns, appears to have left less noticeable scarring on West Africans' psychology than that which endures in the United States.

17 New Secretary-General, London

IN AUTUMN 1981 THE UN was preoccupied with electing a secretary-general. The photograph I have in a drawer somewhere of Waldheim's foxy face, with one arched eyebrow and the hint of either a sneer or sly, ingratiating smile, shows the calculating man he was. Calculating and shrewd as he was he miscalculated towards the end of his second term. Twice he miscalculated disastrously. He campaigned for re-election to a third five years. Although this was without precedent, nothing in the charter ruled it out. He had western support, if only indirectly because the US made it abundantly clear they would never accept, would veto Salim Salim, the rival candidate. Salim had danced in the aisle, the aisle of the General Assembly hall, no exaggeration, after the vote when Taiwan was dethroned and the People's Republic awarded China's seat. The US could never forget.

Waldheim himself was subject to China's initial veto, China arguing that the next Secretary-General should be from the third world. At a dinner honouring the Chinese foreign minister cordial toasts were proposed and Chinese phraseology allowed Waldheim to imagine that China would maintain the veto for two, possibly three rounds of voting, as a matter of principle, before permitting his re-election. He was wrong. China refused to budge on Waldheim, the US on Salim Salim, leaving the Council blocked. That was how Pérez de Cuéllar came to be elected Secretary-General in December 1981. He was a decided outsider, but, after repeated straw polls, proved the only candidate acceptable to the US – friendly Latin American – and China – third world – and not offensive to other permanent members – and who also spoke French fluently.

Waldheim returned home to reap the rewards of international acclaim. He had served the country effectively by making the new, post-second world war, Austria visible on the world stage. He had created the Vienna International Centre as the third major hub of UN activity. From being in the front line, where the western world faced communism, and haunted by Harry Lime, Vienna was becoming a flourishing international city and economically prosperous. Waldheim had realised his ambition to become UN Secretary-

General, to which, according to those who knew him intimately, he aspired even before Austria was admitted to UN membership. To become President of Austria was his other expressed ambition. In campaigning for the presidency he invoked his record on the world stage. He published a book on his international achievements, drafted at Georgetown in DC.

There he made a horrendous blunder. He chose to edit the record of his war service under German command. He stated, not merely implied, that after being wounded on the eastern front, he had spent the remaining time recovering. In fact, he had been assigned as intelligence officer to Heeresgruppe E in Croatia where he was responsible for deportation planning, described as resettlement, which he handled with such administrative competence that he received a decoration. Austrian officers in the German army served under orders – but he could not fail to have been well aware of what his duties involved.

In Austria his political opponents pounced on this dishonesty for their own electoral ends. Internationally, especially in US circles, he was made pariah. That the Austrians elected him nonetheless is almost incidental, the achievement turned to ash in his mouth. He was blocked from entering the US and many other countries; the regal progress of state visits he had envisaged came to nought. A practising Roman Catholic president of a Catholic nation he was received in the Vatican. He also visited Jordan officially, but the style was very different from an earlier arrival in Amman when he was importantly huddled by Crown Prince Hassan into a mini and driven by the prince himself along back roads into town while an assistant arrived by Rolls Royce through the flag-waving main avenue. All for security at a level which was now no longer warranted. This arrival and visit passed so unobtrusively as to escape even media awareness.

Waldheim's dishonesty and the subsequent outrage following public disclosure of his war record had in them something unreal. It was supposedly known in intelligence circles, the Americans and British almost certainly knew, that he had been associated with unsavoury acts while serving with German forces. That had not prevented his original election as Secretary-General; both the US and Britain even contemplated allowing him a third term. He miscalculated by going public, publishing an unnecessary lie, in the heat of a political campaign. Politically astute as he was, calculating and shrewd, I fail to understand why he did not have the wit to adapt his summary of wartime experience, a period in history of which few Austrians were especially proud. Had he written that during the war he was compulsorily enlisted, made aware of horrible events beyond his control, and resolved to dedicate his life to ensuring that such tragedies never recur, none would have challenged it.

Waldheim could not be invited as a former Secretary-General to the UN's fiftieth anniversary in New York. His death in 2007, ending what should have been a remarkable career, attracted more criticism than plaudits. His daughter Liselotte remained with the UN, where she rose honourably through the hierarchy before retiring.

While Waldheim had still been ambitiously clinging to the prospect of re-election as UN secretary-general many of us had already begun speculating as to the most likely successor. The Peruvian ambassador was an outside candidate and emphatically not tipped to win. I was discussing a secretarial appointment with Emilio de Olivares, who processed budget submissions, travel authorisations and personnel action for my division. Emilio was reputed to be a marquis and at least one ex-wife styled herself marchioness; at the UN he was mere 'Mr', a Peruvian national, who occupied a mid-level post. We had almost finished discussing when the phone rang. Emilio answered in Spanish, as if chatting to a friend; 'Come va la vita sexuale?' he asked brightly. 'That was Pérez de Cuéllar,' he said when he stopped speaking and put down the receiver. Emilio said: 'If Pérez de Cuéllar becomes SG, I am made.' How right he was.

Pérez de Cuéllar, against all odds, was elected and appointed Olivares his chief of staff. Emilio loved it. He had the Secretary-General's total confidence and used it to the full. He liked decision making and flaunting his authority. I was in his thirty-eighth floor office one morning to discuss a routine matter when the secretary interrupted with yet another call. His assistant was summoned and Emilio explained that the Secretary-General's choice (when he said 'the Secretary-General's choice' you never knew whether that meant Pérez de Cuéllar's decision or his own) for London had fallen through. Julian Grenfell, Lord Grenfell in fact, a delightful Englishman handling external relations at the World Bank, was being considered for the vacant post. The post, originally director of the UN Information Centre, amounted to UN representation in the United Kingdom and Pérez de Cuéllar wanted it given greater prominence: to function more like an embassy. Grenfell accepted, then regretfully had to decline having discovered that his several children would be ineligible for education grants. Olivares turned from his assistant to ask my views. Did I have any candidates to suggest? We discussed various names. Emilio, suddenly, said: 'What about you? Might you be interested?'

Since I was in a senior post with real responsibility, a full director in the Secretary-General's office, incidentally with a magnificent office on the 38th floor overlooking Manhattan, I had no obvious incentive, and certainly no professional reason to move. But for family reasons it made sense. To Emilio I said: 'Possibly.' He liked snap decisions. Before I could say more he summoned the Under-Secretary-General for Administration and began dictating a memorandum. I remember the start precisely; he began: 'The Secretary-General has decided to appoint Erik Jensen ...' He considered it settled. I interrupted, I had to, 'Look, Emilio,' I said, 'I am interested. But you must give me till tomorrow to decide. At least I have to tell my wife.'

That evening I asked my wife where she wanted to retire. 'I don't know,' she said vaguely, certainly thinking the query premature from a man not yet fifty. I persisted. She became irritated. Then I said: 'This is a serious question and I am asking it for a serious reason,' which seemed to irritate her further. Finally: 'Well, I suppose England, or perhaps the south of France.' 'America?' I ventured. 'No,' she did not think that was where she wanted to retire. 'What's all this about, anyway?' I said: 'I've been offered London, and now I shall accept.'

My son was just eight-years-old, the age at which boys in England traditionally enter preparatory school prior to public school. He had been accepted for Eton conditional on his passing the entrance examination. Neither of his parents wished to send a sensitive eight year old to board the other side of the Atlantic. But without intensive preparation in all relevant subjects, including Latin, even Greek, he was unlikely to succeed in entering a first class English public school at thirteen; American schooling lacked the range and discipline.

To be honest, it was less Eton that mattered than the prospect of his achieving a place at Oxford. My own Oxford experience, and exposure to other universities, European and American, had convinced me that Oxford was uniquely enjoyable as well as providing the best of education and, because of the college system, a wonderfully varied circle of friends. If some of that concern sounds old-fashioned, or snobbish, it also reflects a problem facing most expatriates. Of all my European colleagues at the UN, whether British, French, Scandinavian or Spanish, only one had a child who after receiving both primary and secondary education in the US, even at the international school, chose to be European in Europe. American education is brilliantly designed, after all, to take immigrant material of any aspiration, hue or texture, and mould Americans. Once a fully-fashioned American you tend to marry within the tribe, live as trained, and reproduce on tribal lands. Hence the question I put to my wife. When time came she would surely want to retire where her married children were and any grandchildren.

London promised more than it delivered. Not London's fault precisely. In fact, I enjoyed London, where I had grown up and gone to school and had friends and relations, and England. That very first morning I was met at the airport, after an overnight flight, and taken to a friend's garden for breakfast. It was June. Flowers bloomed everywhere, birds sang to distraction, sunshine fell through overhanging branches onto an impeccably stripe-mown lawn. Later, after meeting near St James's park someone I had not seen in years, we had a pint of bitter beer. This was good old England. As for the children's education, that too met every expectation. My son received excellent preparatory schooling, passed with distinction into his public school and won a place at Oxford and a first class degree. My daughter did as brilliantly and after Oxford went on to ever higher things. Unfortunately, the professional aspect was far from fully realised. Pérez de Cuéllar's ambitious plans foundered on Washington's incessant harassment and, more specifically, the UN financial crisis. America's mood had become anti-international, anti-multilateral, anti-UN. The General Assembly's resolution equating Zionism with racism may have gratified Arab opinion and mollified Palestinian frustration but it infuriated America: as an affront to public and political opinion. We were made to pay the price.

The United States retaliated, delaying or withholding its contribution to the assessed budget. Posts had to be cut, projects remain unfunded. The Heritage Foundation, a far right-wing think tank in Washington, well financed, issued and distributed diatribe upon diatribe assaulting one aspect of UN activity after another. Presented like serious research papers they chose only such selected facts as suited their argument. UN published responses, sounding plaintive, defensive, almost inevitably came too late. And the UN could hardly retaliate by taking the offensive against its critic and the power behind it.

They were bad years for the UN. Made worse by failure to act in the catastrophic war between Iraq and Iran due to continuing gridlock in the Security Council, where the United States and the Soviet Union faced off each other in cold warfare. World events conspired to sabotage even a modest effort to salvage something of the UN image. I invited influential media personalities to a high-level seminar, and they accepted; the US chose that morning in April 1986 to bomb Libya thus purloining the media. Both the US and Britain withdrew from UNESCO. Western newspapers rarely mentioned the UN, except to criticise or mock. When at my urging Rosemary Righter, a well-respected journalist in London, wrote sympathetically about UN development work, the editor superimposed a sarcastic headline. Pérez de Cuéllar was so little known to the public that no one in the street recognised him. He was so little known that Scotland Yard even refused my routine request for security on the grounds that there was no known threat to his person. Only the few UNA supporters showed any interest in his visits. So much for image projection.

Pérez de Cuéllar came through London often. Concorde flew him to London and convenient connections worldwide. His wife happened also to have a married daughter living in Chelsea. I came to know him on many journeys to and from Heathrow. He could be taciturn; he could also be talkative and surprisingly frank about the personalities with whom he had to deal, including senior UN officials. Political appointees had their own priorities, and were reluctant to put too many eggs in the fragile UN basket. Some barely understood what the UN was.

One head of public information, whose background was in advertising, proposed a giant neon sign on the UN roof to display the latest Security Council news and items of interest. Intelligence, sensitivity and experience were all important, but to Pérez de Cuéllar loyalty mattered as much if not more. Not all those in responsible posts at the UN put loyalty to the Secretary-General first. During those impossible years he aged and aged. I always remember his arriving after a many hour, exhausting flight following upon long, exhausting and inconclusive talks in Iraq. Disappointment, frustration showed in his face, which was colourless, not even ashen. He wanted only to be left alone. Back in New York he was admitted to hospital for quadruple bypass surgery.

Less dramatic and, of course, less significant were my efforts to project better understanding of the UN throughout the United Kingdom and in Ireland where I was also accredited. I was early convinced that giving talks to the converted at UNA gatherings served only as preaching to the faithful, almost without exception elderly, and dwindling in number. On one occasion when I invited questions after

*In my newly presented
UN London office*

finishing my speech a wispy-grey-haired woman in the front row indicated she had something to ask. 'Of course,' I said, genuinely interested in what she might say. In a high-pitched voice came 'May I go now?'

The more active, and youthful idealists, were drawn to high profile single issue causes. Unilateral disarmament, in particular, attracted many. My own experience at non-governmental disarmament gatherings in Geneva had taught me that, however nobly motivated, unilateral disarmament efforts tended to rely on insufficient knowledge and grasp of military reality; they were not likely to further the end of the cold war. This was not a cause to which I could commit myself. More objective, more open, more fertile, by far, I thought, was the university world. Young people, their idealism not fully focused, were receptive to alternative ideas, to persuasion and willing to argue. I began accepting all invitations to lecture, conduct seminars, and engage with students. And found this as stimulating as it was challenging.

Hammarskjöld had spoken in Oxford's Sheldonian Theatre and Pérez de Cuéllar aspired also to lecture there. Through contacts in my old university it was arranged, for the month of May, in 1986. Adam Roberts, who had just succeeded Hedley Bull as professor of international relations, organised the details. Attendance was modest, and Pérez de Cuéllar was never an impressive public speaker, especially in English, but he was a reflective man, an intellectual with academic qualifications, whose talk, whose ideas about the secretary-generalship were important. The lecture was edited for publication, and became the catalyst for a series of other lectures by eminent UN personalities, and a book. The Cyril Foster bequest, little known and with limited resources, funded some costs, including an agreeable dinner at Balliol. Raymond Carr, warden of St Antony's, presided. He was very relaxed, approaching retirement, and Carr being a venerated historian of Spain he and Perez were at ease. The wine was excellent. No toasts, bar one, when the warden of St Antony's raised his glass to propose: 'Cyril Foster – whoever he was.'

The UN Secretary-General generated more interest in Scotland and Wales and I was able to organise visits. Both in Edinburgh and Cardiff he attracted a large and appreciative audience. In Wales support for international organisation dated from the League of Nations. The rich Welsh industrialist Lord Davies of Llandinam, personally committed to the internationalist principles of the covenant and the League, bequeathed a fortune to establish a centre housed in an imposing building, which reflected the style, period and hopes of the Palais des Nations in Geneva: the Temple of Peace. His endowment subsidised the continuing work of the Welsh Centre for International Affairs. Director in my day was Bill Davies, no relative, of course, of Lord Davies in a land where many share the same surname. Bill, energetic, focused and with excellent connections throughout Wales, arranged brief speaking tours for me two or three times a year. We went in rotation to different parts of the principality. I was invariably received with courtesy and respect and honoured with Welsh lamb by local dignitaries, who made me feel welcome even when they lapsed into speaking Welsh between themselves.

In north Wales the mayor assured me of a good turn-out as we walked over to the meeting. Neat rows of seating occupied a large room. Near the door as we entered I noticed an interpretation booth; the only other furniture was on a low platform at the far end where a table stood and two chairs. People were rapidly filling seats throughout as the mayor directed me forward to the dais. In the very front row, right in the middle, sat an impressive elderly gentleman, a cloak slung loosely about his shoulders. He looked hard at me while the mayor introduced their distinguished speaker, in English followed by a few words in Welsh. I rose to speak. No sooner had I started than the impressive man stood up, in the centre of the first row and, with a theatrical flourish, threw his cloak about him, marched towards the corridor out of the hall. An air of embarrassment was obvious. The mayor turned towards me with an awkward smile. To make a joke of it, I broke off in mid-sentence and said: 'I would apologise for what I have said, but I haven't really said anything yet.' Just enough for a polite laugh. I continued with my speech. Afterwards the mayor was profusely apologetic. He much regretted the impoliteness shown me. Did I know who it was? No idea. It was a very well-known Welsh poet, R.S. Thomas. He was fanatical about the use of the Welsh language. Whenever present at a public lecture, and he made a point of being present whenever possible, he demonstrated if it was not delivered in Welsh. There was no offence to me personally. Out of curiosity I asked the mayor in which language Thomas wrote his poetry. In English.

When the cold war approached its ending the United Nations moved closer to centre stage. Pérez de Cuéllar was able to play a significant part in the concluding days of the Iran-Iraq conflict, his role respected, his name known. In Britain people recognised the name, even the face, pointed him out, actually asked for his signature when he appeared in public. Scotland Yard did not hesitate to maintain full security. He was sympathetically received in government circles, and when in London officially there was a meeting at 10 Downing Street. I accompanied Pérez de Cuéllar to see Mrs Thatcher several times. Relations were cordial. She liked him, it was apparent. She had been impressed by his conduct when the Falklands dispute erupted. He, newly elected secretary-general and a Latin American, had been scrupulously fair in seeking a solution. He betrayed no pro-Argentinian bias and came close to achieving a compromise acceptable to Britain. Mrs Thatcher, who had identified Gorbachev as someone with whom to do business and approved of Pérez de Cuéllar, saw an enhanced role for the UN after the cold war. She discussed a range of issues, informally. The encounters were understood to be confidential and private, one plus one.

Pérez de Cuéllar was placed in a large sofa with me to his far right. The Prime Minister sat in a chair opposite and was accompanied by either Geoffrey Howe or Charles Powell. Neither I nor Charles Powell was expected to speak. Geoffrey Howe, in a different class, might add to what the PM said, on occasion butting in. If she disagreed, she said so sharply. Once she slapped him over the wrist, with: 'No, Geoffrey, no.' The Foreign Secretary smiled weakly, and filed that for later. She resented contradiction, seemed always so sure of her opinion – her strength and ultimately her fault line. The schoolmistress, she acted and looked as though she might be head mistress of a well-disciplined girls' school, with her hair set and sharp nose. But she was not unattractive. Those who met her in person all testify to those beautiful blue eyes.

Mrs Thatcher greeting Pérez de Cuéllar at 10 Downing Street

Despite being at ease with Pérez de Cuéllar Maggie Thatcher was no natural multilateralist. Two British ambassadors to the UN helped in internationalising her instinctively narrower horizon. First was Tony Parsons, permanent representative in New York during the war over the Falklands. He had already been in post for a time, in fact, was scheduled to retire, and was widely liked and respected. That made a difference, that and his grasp and experience of Security Council workings, when it came to defending

Britain in a forum not traditionally well disposed to the exercise of imperial power and its residue. The United Kingdom achieved its diplomatic objective, to the surprise not only of Argentina. Military success followed, but the diplomatic advantage mattered, and Tony Parsons received the credit he deserved. When his retirement came, briefly postponed contrary to rigid Foreign Office practice, the Prime Minister made him number ten's foreign policy adviser. Anyone else in that position would likely have infuriated the foreign office. Parsons managed not to. And he successfully realigned some of Mrs Thatcher's reactions on international liberal-tending issues. She always listened with respect to his advice, he told me, without necessarily agreeing. On one occasion she reacted more negatively than usual, saying: 'I'm glad I'm not from your class, Tony.' 'What do you mean, Prime Minister?' 'Always seeing the other chap's point of view.' Come to think of it that was what a classical public school education inculcated: a well formulated Greek period, rather than a sentence, had the particle 'men' inserted near the beginning and a 'de' at the second half. You were taught not to translate them literally, they stood for 'on the one hand' and 'on the other hand.'

Crispin Tickell was the other ambassador to influence thinking in number ten. Crispin earlier in his career had been a visiting fellow at Harvard's Weatherhead Institute for International Affairs. In addition to attending lectures, participating in seminars and generally interacting, fellows were urged to write a paper. Crispin wrote on the wider implications of climate change: the political impact, refugee flows and so forth. These concerns reached beyond the high-minded non-governmental constituency then associated with environmental matters. Crispin claimed that it was he who 'greened' Mrs Thatcher.

She emerged more sympathetic to the UN and was favourably disposed towards Pérez de Cuéllar when his second term as secretary-general was about to expire. The last time I saw him with Mrs Thatcher she received him with obvious warmth but he opened the interview by saying firmly: 'Don't even think of asking me to stand again.' Britain had no choice but to accept his decision.

In December 1991 the UN found itself with a new Secretary-General, Boutros Boutros-Ghali. Boutros was not Britain's preferred candidate. For one reason, as Crispin Tickell was widely quoted as saying, 'We think he has been 69 for too long.' Boutros was close, very close to the French and much preferred speaking French to English, though so, as a matter of fact, had Pérez de Cuéllar.

18 General Assembly and other affairs

BEFORE LEAVING OFFICE Pérez de Cuéllar summoned me back to New York. The public information professionals always wanted one of their own in the plum London job and the decline in UN finances ruled out developing the office politically and diplomatically. My personal circumstances were also changed. Both children had been absorbed into the English educational system at excellent schools. One was already a boarder, the other soon to become one. General Assembly Affairs, where I was appointed director, proved an interesting experience. For two or three years. Not a post, though, where one would wish to spend a long career. It was demanding, all too often also boring. General Assembly presidents varied. I enjoyed the two with whom I worked most closely: de Marco of Malta and Shihabi of Saudi Arabia.

The presidency panders to self-importance. It looks grand; the president appears important seated at the high rostrum, presiding over heads of major states. In reality the presidency confers little or no power, even influence. It depends on its own diplomatic mission for support, and has no dedicated budget. It looms larger for incumbents in their national life than internationally. The Assembly is important nonetheless, not for endless hackneyed speechifying, spouting of platitudes, prolific dispersal of exaggerated compliments requiring reciprocation, the tedium of routine voting, but because it takes place. Heads of State, Heads of Government, foreign ministers and other national representatives mill around the UN building. For two or three weeks the world's political decision makers are gathered together with unrestricted mutual access. Informal contact, apparently unintended encounters, unofficial meetings with countries ostracised from polite international society as well as traditional business all become possible, almost mandatory.

The opening of my first General Assembly session in September 1992 was exceptional. The Assembly hall bulged at the seams to hear President George Bush, representing the host country, deliver his historic speech endorsing Gorbachev's new world order. Everyone applauded, discreet diplomats as loudly as enthusiasts in the public gallery. To all of us the world seemed more wholesome, a healthier body, less self-destructive. Conflicts that had endured for years, even decades, had become susceptible to resolution. Euphoria prevailed. The Soviet Union became Russia and ceased to vie for global supremacy as leader of the communist bloc. The United States emerged as undisputed champion not only of the west but of free market democracy.

On the General Assembly podium, New York

History, as Francis Fukuyama claimed, in that sense came to an end. Some, more realist, without wanting to be negative, cautioned against excessive optimism. That winter I was invited to deliver the commencement address at Richmond College, the American university in London, and I spoke about the new world order. The President thanked me profusely. It was a perfect speech, which he wished to publish, but might I not have been less guarded in my optimism. With the benefit of hindsight I was, if anything, too optimistic.

After the president of the United States came other heads of state. None attracted quite the same attendance, security measures and coverage, but they were days of frantic activity. The General Assembly team had not a second to spare. Just as I readied to enter the hall one morning I was irritated by yet another interruption. A Russian ambassador wished to see me. It was apparently not the Russian ambassador, the permanent representative, but a senior member of their delegation. Nothing on the speakers' list or the agenda suggested an urgent Russian intervention, and it was too late to change. 'He wants to see you now,' I was told, 'He insists on seeing you personally.' 'Well, show him in.'

In walked Vladimir Lobachev. 'Erik,' he said, giving me a classical Russian bear hug, "'ow are you?' I was well and how was he. 'Am here for few days only, with Ludmilla.' 'You must come,' I said, 'both of you, and have a drink with me, and we can talk.' Vladimir and Ludmilla came to my apartment next day for an extraordinary reunion. Years before, in Geneva, much as we manifestly liked each other in the office, he had been prohibited under the old Soviet system from accepting any invitation from me or from inviting me home. Even when he arrived one ghastly February night, aware that I was coming down with flu, to offer me 'his mother's pills' he would not move inside the front-door. 'Everything changed' and he beamed. He had had an embassy in Africa, in the Central African Republic – not, I discovered, when I was there – and was now in Moscow. 'Please to visit.'

Such moments brought rare delight to our daily routine as the division responsible for smooth running of the Assembly. Sitting on the podium next to the President, as either I or the relevant Under-Secretary-General was required to do, offered a splendid view of the hall, which was fun at first. Packed for star speakers, but as day followed day, week followed week, attendance thinned and the speeches grew increasingly repetitive and boring. When necessary, Vice-Presidents deputised for the elected President who was not expected to preside in person over every session. Vice-Presidents were chosen from all regional UN groups; most welcomed the photo opportunity in presiding, presumably to impress constituents back home. My task was to organise a Vice-President whenever the President announced that he was unavailable.

Geographical sensitivity was essential, balance between regions and countries within regions. Occasionally this caused difficulty. Some Vice-Presidents were reluctant to serve: they had better things to do than sit on the podium pretending to take interest in the rambling oration of some unimportant national representative – on a peripheral issue. One Vice-President, whom I knew as Egypt's energetic and effective ambassador, was always evasive. I had to insist. As he took his seat he turned his head away from the microphone and asked: 'What am I supposed to do here? I can't lobby and I can't smoke.' Having done his duty he refused to repeat the honour. He left New York to become Egypt's foreign minister, and later Secretary-General of the Arab League, lobbying actively in both capacities – and probably smoking his favourite small cigars.

Di Marco as President aspired to a 'Presidency with a purpose' and bequeathed a copiously illustrated book of that title. Samir Shihabi, as his legacy, had ambitions to create within the secretariat an office specifically dedicated to support the President. He invited me to head it, at an exalted level. Flattered though I was and attracted to the idea of leading a unit outside the established hierarchy, I never expected the proposal to materialise. Nor, to be honest, did I think such a new office warranted. It can be difficult when personal interest diverges from what you believe right for the organisation. Shihabi's plan was doomed further by timing.

Pérez de Cuéllar had been succeeded as Secretary-General by Boutros-Ghali and the experienced Egyptian Boutros-Ghali was not overly impressed by Shihabi's Saudi self-importance, not least since he was Palestinian born. Boutros-Ghali, still close to the US, was taking advice from the newly appointed American Under-Secretary-General. Ron Spiers, who had been responsible for administration in the State Department, argued forcefully for a severe reduction in top level appointments, the amalgamation of departments, and stream-lining chains of command. A presidential office was out of the question in these circumstances; In 1992 the General Assembly affairs division itself became exposed to possible amalgamation, absorption or other restructuring.

During that uncomfortable spell before we knew how 'restructuring' would affect us personally, political attention focused on Boutros-Ghali's proposed 'Agenda for Peace'. Given all that happened later it can be hard to remember with what hope, what expectation Boutros-Ghali's tenure began. The Security

Council was convened at summit level, which had never occurred before. Heads of State in most cases, with one or two heads of government where the head of state had only constitutional powers, accepted to be in New York on 31 January 1992 to formulate a worthy mandate for the UN in a new world order.

President George Bush was coming, President Yeltsin, President Mitterand, King Hassan II of Morocco – Morocco having been elected to a two-year non-permanent seat on the Council. The rotating presidency fell to the United Kingdom, therefore John Major, as Prime Minister. Security was at peak. The chamber and adjoining corridors swarmed with bulky men, dressed in ill-fitting suits which bulged beneath the armpit, adorned with visible hearing aids and talking to themselves. Only they had unrestricted access, everyone else was rigorously excluded, bar a handful of us who were individually asked to meet heads of state on arrival and ensure their orderly move to the Security Council chamber. As director my task was to be in the salon where all would be assembled, to greet them, and keep count of who was there. I found myself trying to make conversation to President Yeltsin when President Bush entered, walked straight towards Yeltsin, and said:

'Boris, you're looking great, Boris.'

To which, with some interpreter's aid, Yeltsin replied: 'Looking good yourself, George.'

'Yeah,' Bush said, 'Everyone gets a touch of flu now and then. I'm fine.' He had recently returned from a state visit to Japan where at the televised banquet he fell sick in his soup.

The conversation becoming personal, I withdrew. Major, I noticed, was looking about him. To me he said: 'I like to start the meeting on time.'

A quick head-count showed two still missing. Mitterand had not arrived, nor had King Hassan. I called over the security guard on duty who confirmed that both were in the building. Then what are they waiting for? At that moment both stepped in, almost simultaneously, each deferring to the other: 'after you'. They had been manoeuvring, I was told, to be last; in diplomatic protocol the most important arrives last. That was the only time I saw Mitterand in the skin – and what wrinkled skin. Only once in my life had I seen a man equally wrinkled: the poet W.H. Auden. Auden, of course, smoked endlessly, had smoked all his life. Mitterand, apparently, had advanced prostrate cancer, and was being kept alive by medication. Always the exception, the President of France had someone with him: the AdC armed with the button to France's nuclear weapon.

Fanfare surrounded the Security Council, other UN reform was more pedestrian. Reform, which the Americans made a condition for paying their budget contribution, meant reorganising, usually combining departments as well as reducing top level posts. General Assembly affairs was to be amalgamated with services to ECOSOC, not altogether irrational. Details were being discussed when Ambassador Reed, Joseph Verner Reed, approached me. (He objected strongly to being called Joe; Joseph was for intimates, JVR for others wishing to be friendly.) He was seriously rich, with a house in privileged Greenwich, Connecticut, surrounded by an estate so expansive no other building could be seen. He told me later that the land was being donated to the American Audubon society to ensure its inviolability.

With Ambassador Joseph Verner Reed,
former United States Chief of Protocol

JVR was a Rockefeller republican, the liberal wing of the party, committed to idealistic America, and he loved the UN. He had served as US ambassador in Morocco, at the mission to the UN, and as chief of protocol under President Bush – his least proud moment, he told me, when his 'very tall President' spoke followed by a 'very small Queen' at the same lectern leaving only her hat visible to the audience. To his delight he was back at the UN as Under-Secretary-General for public affairs. He was close to the elder Bush White House, mostly Yalies like himself, and he admired Boutros. His role was to function as an informal link with Washington in addition to his official responsibilities.

JVR invited me to be his deputy. One task was to begin planning for the fiftieth anniversary of the UN: Boutros-Ghali hoped to use this occasion to focus world opinion on his ideas for making the UN a lynchpin of the new world order. Working alongside JVR was always colourful. He filled the reception area with pieces of art, some very good, from his own collection, some idiosyncratic. In his office he displayed a complete set of American state flags and predecessor flags to the stars and stripes, including one of a coiled snake under the motto 'Don't step on me' – undoubtedly the flag that motivated John Bolton, his own ambassador's flag and more, and in pride of place, the rocking-chair that once belonged to John F. Kennedy. Whenever occasion warranted he exhibited in the office open plan space an impressive array of Moroccan rugs. JVR's strength was personal relations and he relished serving in 'This House of Peace' as he habitually called the UN. He took pride in representing the Secretary-General in various contexts; some more substantive functions he preferred delegating to me. So I found myself coordinating assistance to those affected by the Chernobyl disaster. Ukraine, Byelorussia and Russia all needed help in varying degrees. They had been given false hope by an unrealistic aid programme presented at a UN donor conference when critics singled out prioritising an appeal for reconstruction of a brewery. The result: international assistance fell drastically short of expectation, as they complained to me in Kiev. I was reminded of the Comoros and the presidential aircraft, which we had successfully rerouted.

The Ukrainians recited again the depressing saga of destruction, contamination, and, not least, the unknown longer term consequences for human health. Childhood leukaemia showed a marked increase, some experts maintained, though others challenged the figures. The airmen involved in dowsing the exploding reactor with concrete had been posted to different corners of the Russian empire to minimise the impact on statistics; no one could be sure what had become of them. The evidence of Chernobyl itself remained for all to see, provided one was dressed in protective clothing.

Only wildlife benefitted, birds and small animals flourished in the absence of human beings, though pessimists believed these too would be deformed, birds unable to fly, deer born with three legs. Fortunately, the doomsayers proved wrong. Facts are hard to establish and much remains unclear, but the worst prophecies were never realised. Although the area surrounding the reactors would take decades or longer to recuperate, Kiev and the Ukraine were poised to move on. Kiev is an ancient city, founded by Vikings, who sailed up-river; a statue commemorates the event. Like much of Europe the country has known persecution, turbulence and survived. At the monastery a blond monk, who had continued to watch over medieval reliquiae throughout communist rule, looked to the future. I left the monastery feeling confident that the Ukraine would emerge from this latest crisis, as it had from other crises in its history.

In 1993 a bombshell from which there was no escaping hit JVR when George Bush failed to win re-election. The incumbent, the heroic president who mobilised a great international coalition, whose victorious forces expelled Iraqi invaders from Kuwait, had been defeated in the polls, denied a second term. The new president was Bill Clinton, a democrat. Joseph Reed now belonged to the wrong party. He had lost privileged access in Washington, with a new democratic administration, and knew his time was up. Ted Sorensen, famous for drafting Kennedy's historic speech about asking not what your country can do for you but what you can do for your country, remained a force in democrat circles – and he had a younger wife who wanted work at the UN. The US proposed Mrs Sorensen to succeed Reed.

Personal chemistry matters more in public life, and at the UN, than many realise. I felt no antipathy towards Mrs Sorensen, but that I was known to have so cordial relations with JVR militated against me being her deputy, so it seemed to her team. That I shared many democrat values was immaterial. When responsibility for Chernobyl and other duties were being reassigned it looked as if my career had abruptly peaked before the official retirement age of sixty. I was just fifty-nine years old. Personnel, now Human Resources, inscribed me in a seminar for imminent retirees to talk about health care in old age, keeping busy, thinking through where to live and how to live on a pension. It was bad enough being fifty-nine – with chronic lymphocytic leukaemia. Leukaemia had been diagnosed, by chance, two years earlier.

I had been asked at short notice to become conference secretary at the first major gathering called to discuss an international convention on climate change. Surprisingly, the United States offered to host the conference in Washington. Chimney stackers and tree huggers battled each other, while delegates from India and elsewhere challenged the right of three car per family America to condemn them to riding bicycles. It was a difficult conference, but important and it opened the way for further meetings leading eventually to Kyoto.

The prospect of running such a gathering with a persistent and unsavoury cough had led me to the UN medical service. I asked to see any available doctor and was directed to Dr Pasquier – to my great good fortune. Dr Pasquier looked me over and sent me for a blood test, which surprised me since all I had expected was cough linctus or something to suck. That afternoon, it was a Friday, I returned to Dr Pasquier for a prescription. She invited me to be seated, speaking very calmly and quietly. I suspected the worst. 'I think you have leukaemia,' she said. The blood analysis showed a greatly elevated white cell count. She had asked for a test having noticed, without physical examination, enlarged glands in my neck. Much later she told me she had been training to specialise in haematology till marriage intervened: that was why she had noticed what few general practitioners might have spotted. 'I can't be absolutely certain,' Dr Pasquier continued, 'there could, just possibly, be some other explanation.' I was in a state of shock.

As she said, there might be some other explanation; I had no experience then of assessing white cell counts. And my priority was preparation for the conference which I was having to organise.

'You need to see a specialist,' she said, 'they may want to check your bone marrow.'

'If it isn't too urgent,' I said, 'I'd prefer waiting till just after the conference which begins in a week's time.'

'I don't think it advisable to wait,' Dr Paquier said, paused, then 'I've already made an appointment for you at Memorial' – Sloane-Kettering, New York's well-known cancer hospital.

'When is it for?'

'Monday morning, at 9 a.m.'

I think I gulped. I know I departed, without linctus or cough drops, to spend a difficult weekend, alone. Most of the time I painted. The picture, I am proud to say, was not bad. I wrote camouflaged letters to both children, trying not to sound maudlin and without giving obvious cause for alarm. Monday morning I set off for Memorial in the cold, damp bleakness of January in New York city.

At any time of year few cancer hospitals are designed to lift spirits. Patients, in varying stages of disfiguring illness, were wheeled about, or staggered on walking frames. Dr M examined me and confirmed the diagnosis of CLL; he dispatched me for bone marrow analysis, to be sure, he said, although there was no doubt in his mind. 'You are an educated man and, rather than my explaining in simplified language about the disease, probably prefer to read these.' He handed me off-prints of two articles from medical journals. 'Do ask if there is anything you don't fully understand.' And as I was leaving 'I'll send the results of the bone marrow test to Dr Pasquier.'

Bone marrow analysis has a reputation as painful, and it is unpleasant, but not nearly as bad as I had been led to believe. They stick a large hypodermic into the lower spine, and, yes, that hurts, then suck out a marrow sample. Afterwards it felt bruised but nothing worse. Inevitably, the test results bore out the diagnosis. I had leukaemia. The learned papers spelled out in discouraging detail the nature of the disease and my prognosis. The author of one, a specialist in CLL, worked at a hospital in nearby Long Island. When I asked Dr M whether a second opinion was warranted he referred me to Dr Kanti Rai. Dr Rai studied my test results and the further monitoring of blood counts and abnormal cells; he concluded that the diagnosis was not in doubt. Bone marrow transplant offered the only cure. Even if a compatible donor could be found (my sister had sweetly volunteered), I was too old. Maximum age was fifty-five; later than that the vital organs were liable to fail after being immobilised during the transplant. Chemotherapy was an option when the disease reached its advanced stage, but by-effects apart, this should be a last resort since chemotherapy was usually effective only at first. Dr Rai, who had my file in front of him, looked up, over the top of his glasses: 'At what age do you retire at the UN?'

'Sixty.'

'Is there anything particular that you still want to accomplish?'

I said there was a book I had been intending to write.

'How long would that take you?' he asked.

'Maybe two years.'

'Then you may wish to take early retirement.'

He talked soothingly about what an interesting life I had surely had, and that all lives came to an end, something that I as an intelligent person would understand perfectly well.

I saw no reason to broadcast my illness, nor was I secretive – doctor's appointments could never be kept secret in a close-knit office. A friend inevitably told another. One morning Irene called. Irene I knew but very slightly, a former colleague, who always wore dark glasses long before this was considered a fashion statement, and behaved weirdly. This was attributed, whether true or not, to her Polish Jewish origins and unspeakable wartime experience. Why Irene should call I could not imagine. She happened to have heard I had leukaemia. How she did not say, but she was always receptive to gossip. She had some advice to give me, a Chinese herbalist she knew had worked miracles for a friend of hers and he might help me. Spurious medicine reminded me of back street abortionists, and I had no automatic confidence in an aged Chinese, with one absurdly long hair sprouting from a mole on his inscrutable face, mumbling phoney Chinese-American magic. Irene gave me a name and I thanked her. That was that as far as I was concerned. Days later she called back. I had my secretary explain that I was in a meeting. Another day or two, same again. The next time she phoned twice, three times in the course of a morning, and I answered. I promised to contact the Chinese herbalist, if only to spare my secretary the embarrassment of further calls.

The Chinese herbalist was anything but his stereotype. He was a graduate of the London School of Economics, a statistician, with a westernized name, who worked for the UN, clean shaven, youthful looking, and very convincing. Chinese medicine was Keith Tong's passion, and as well as qualifying in statistics, in London, he qualified, in China, in traditional medicine. He practised in his own time. Keith was serious. He examined the blood analyses, cell counts and detailed diagnosis from Memorial before studying my tongue, despite my embarrassment at sticking it out, and checking the slipperiness of my pulse. Mine was a case, he concluded, where he might be able to help, but it would not be quick. Chinese medicine treated each individual patient rather than assuming that a particular disease always merited the same treatment, as in the west. Herbs were slower to act than the distilled, fabricated drugs customarily injected in America and he would need to monitor the effect of different herbal remedies. Patience was essential, and commitment to continue treatment for a longish period of time. I never had been one to expect instant gratification, I said I would willingly try.

Less keen I might have been had I realised what the course of treatment entailed. The plastic bag given me contained a jumble of dried vegetable matter and other strange items, including a desiccated caterpillar. Every single morning a portion was to be soaked, then simmered until the resulting liquid had been reduced to a glassful. It had to be watched while it took its time. It smelled ghastly. And so it tasted. Having assured Keith that I would abide by his course of treatment I dutifully rose early every morning, to boil up, like the witches in Macbeth, my sinister concoction. The aftertaste I dulled with tea and coffee. For weeks, three, four, six, eight, the white cell count, regularly monitored by the medical service, continued to mount and the number of abnormal cells. The need for chemotherapy was almost upon me when, in the course of one week, the test results stabilised and over a fortnight declined. Only very slightly lower at first, but they were lower. And so it continued, slowly, over several months. Keith changed the composition of my herb bag, not that I knew much difference, and gradually diminished the dose. After just over a year treatment was prescribed for every other day before being further reduced to twice weekly. Two years from the original diagnosis Dr

M at Memorial asked for another bone marrow sample, and was amazed. Dr Pasquier smiled: 'You should not imagine yourself cured,' she said, but I could be considered in remission.

So unusual was the case, and so unwilling western medics to concede that I had been successfully treated by a Chinese herbalist, that they preferred to attribute my recovery to the one in a million instance of spontaneous healing. My history was recorded in the medical literature, where I appeared anonymously as 'an elderly gentleman', together with a guarded description of Keith's medicine. I insisted that Keith Tong receive any credit – and whatever lucrative patent might arise from his drug.

19 Final mission: Western Sahara

My health had ceased to worry me personally until summoned to the thirty-eighth floor about a mission. I dreaded being medically disqualified. The mission was to Cambodia, for the elections, and I was proposed as deputy to the Secretary-General's representative, Yasushi Akashi. Japan was playing a leading role for regional and other reasons, not least financial, and the head of mission was to be Japanese. Akashi was a UN career official recently elevated to the political level, who benefited from Japan's burgeoning profile in international affairs; he spoke good English and knew the UN. The deputy's nationality was less circumscribed. For an hour or more I sat with Yasushi, whom I had known for a time but not well, and discussed Cambodia. I knew south-east Asia though not Indo-China, I had mission experience and spoke French, my strengths were political and diplomatic. Akashi saw his own strengths as similar to mine and he needed a deputy to relieve him of administrative responsibility. Much as I hankered after a mission assignment, and Indo-China appealed, I doubted that I would enjoy relegation to a purely administration role. It became immaterial that the medical service might have declared me medically unfit.

By early 1993 I was preoccupied, not by health concerns but by the breaking up of JVR's old office, my intermediate future and the looming prospect of retiring in December that year. I had recently been invited to deliver the winter commencement address at Connecticut University's central campus. The president, while telling me of his decision to publish my talk as an occasional paper, mentioned the reciprocal arrangements he was developing in Syracusa, in Sicily, and I was asked to speak at a conference on 'Peace through Education'. In London, on the way to Sicily, I received an urgent telephone call. Jean-Claude Aime, the Secretary-General's chief of staff, came on the line to enquire whether I would be interested in MINURSO. MINURSO, I knew, related to Western Sahara and I had read reports about the Polisario refugee camps. That was about all. I would be appointed 'President de la Commission d'Identification'. Meaning what precisely? 'Number two, deputy head of mission, Jean-Claude said. And the level? 'Assistant Secretary-General.' Here was a mission, a mission with uncertain prospects it was true, but a challenge. I said 'yes'.

The highest level in the UN career service was full director. Beyond career posts lay a top echelon of political appointees, originally conceived as corresponding to ministers. These, at the Assistant Secretary-General and Under-Secretary-General level, were contractual appointments without security of tenure but also without age limitation. My appointment was proposed for six months to coincide with the Security Council's resolution extending the mission. Longer term perspectives were dim, though I knew from experience how common it was for almost any mission assignment to be prolonged. Medical clearance posed little problem when I mentioned six months to Dr Paquier though I must continue to have monitoring tests, she said, adding: 'Remember you should not consider yourself cured, if in remission.' Briefing was equally non-specific. The UN settlement plan, stalled before really starting, was to be brought to life. My predecessors as head of mission and deputy had left as failures, and accused of lacking impartiality.

Boutros Boutros-Ghali congratulates me

Spain had finally been pressured into surrendering its large west African colony but failed to make provision for an orderly transfer of power. Morocco claimed the former colony as having historically been part of the Sultan's realm. An independence movement, Polisario, founded to expel Spain, refused to countenance incorporation into Morocco. Fighting culminated in the Polisario, together with thousands of its followers, withdrawing into southern Algeria where it declared itself independent as the Sahrawi Arab Democratic Republic. Polisario had not been defeated and with support from Algeria and Libyan arms it mounted successful incursions into both Morocco and Mauritania. Only after years and failed attempts by the OAU to resolve the conflict was a ceasefire agreed to permit a referendum under UN auspices. The proposal: a referendum of self-determination in accordance with traditional UN practice when colonial possessions achieved or were about to be given independence.

The immediate problem lay with identifying those eligible to vote in such a referendum. In most territories it's relatively straightforward to establish who are the authentic inhabitants. The peoples of Western Sahara were nomadic, desert tribes travelling vast distances in search of sparse grazing for their camels and goat herds. They had no fixed address by which to be known. And imperially drawn straight lines on old maps left no trace in the sand to indicate a border crossing or frontier. The Sahrawi tribes wandered wherever the clouds promised rainfall and the light green shoots it would bequeath for their livestock to ingest.

The principal tribes were known to themselves and each other as members of a tribe not a nation state. Identity derived from the tribe, a powerful tribal identity that Polisario sought to supersede by intermingling followers in their quest to create a modern national identity, but Morocco was determined this should be Moroccan not Saharan. In the vast desert region named Spanish Sahara the Spanish had imposed colonial rule over two administrative areas without infringing traditional tribal loyalties. Spain had also colonised enclaves further north, at Tarfaya and, by treaty, at Sidi Ifni in territory recognised as belonging to Morocco. Sahrawi tribes moved throughout this desertic area south of the Draa valley. The tribes based principally in Spanish Sahara maintained that their people and theirs alone had the right to decide on the future status but Morocco argued that this was an unjustified imperial distinction and Sahrawi tribespeople whether living occasionally or mainly south or north of the colonial frontier with ancestral links to the territory should be permitted a voice. A census conducted belatedly before Spain departed included only those in the colony of Spanish Sahara at the time omitting not only Sahrawis from outside the immediate region but the many individuals who were elsewhere in pursuit of education, employment,

Being presented to King Hassan II of Morocco

Meeting Polisario leader Abdel-Aziz

business or for medical treatment.

A UN settlement plan approved by the Security Council was to be implemented with the voluntary cooperation of Morocco and Polisario and both had supposedly agreed. In reality neither side agreed without reservations though the reservations were not officially disclosed. Secretary-general Pérez de Cuéllar seems to have imagined that a compromise solution might be negotiated needing only endorsement. But he retired without achieving any negotiated compromise and having made last minute modifications to the plan producing even more contentious terms for the right to vote. Among diplomats familiar with the issue few had high hopes for implementation.

Two of the secretary-general's special representatives and deputies had resigned by the time I was appointed. Sahabzada Yakub-Khan, an immensely distinguished Pakistani, lieutenant-general, ambassador and foreign minister, was named head of mission. He chose to work out of New York in the ongoing search for political compromise leaving me in charge of the mission in the region, both its military peace-keeping component and civil administration more specifically with responsibility for launching the stalled plan and identification. After less than a year Sahabzada Yakub-Khan abandoned hope of political agreement and withdrew, leaving me as head of the mission.

By then I had formed useful personal relations in Morocco and among Polisario with both parties' responsible individuals as well as with leaders in neighbouring Algeria and Mauritania, officially recognised as interested countries. The mission itself, headquartered at Laayoune, was emerging from a fractious past derived from a bitterly quarrelling leadership. A tragedy, early in my appointment, unexpectedly helped to heal friction.

With Boutros-Ghali on his official visit to the Polisario camps

A light aircraft returning from a medical call to a military observer teamsite crashed on take-off. Pilot and passengers were killed. The force commander wanted a ceremony for the military only but I over-ruled him. The pilot was from our Swiss medical unit, the doctor on board belonged to the Australian military observer contingent and the third to die was a technical expert from the civilian staff, a Norwegian, who had been pressed into dealing with an emergency when he was supposed to be off duty. Nothing exemplified more clearly the oneness of the mission, as I emphasised when addressing the entire staff, military and civilian, in what proved a truly moving event.

With Bachir, Polisario's principal spokesman, in the desert

The UN mission comprised the military, who were mostly deployed at desert team-sites to monitor the cease-fire, and our civil administration, which functioned competently, to which we had added and were training appropriate staff for the identification of potential voters, essential to launching the settlement plan. Working with senior members of the Identification Commission I devised a procedure, for which no precedent existed, to identify those claiming a right to vote and to assess their qualifications under the revised criteria enunciated, at the eleventh hour, by Pérez de Cuéllar.

The criteria satisfied neither Morocco nor Polisario, which made every step contentious. But we eventually developed a formula for identification acceptable to both: each side would present a tribal leader, a sheikh, from the tribal sub-group being identified, for the sheikh to confirm the individual's personal identity and whether he or she qualified under one of the criteria. Both Morocco and Polisario would have official observers as would the OAU. The OAU was mentioned in the settlement plan but Morocco argued forcefully against OAU participation on the grounds that the organisation had prejudged the outcome by recognising Polisario as a member state. It took months of negotiation to achieve a formula permitting an OAU presence, as Polisario insisted, by diluting OAU representation: half nominated by the OAU current president and half from the secretariat. Progress, however, remained blocked by Polisario's unbudging refusal to accept Pérez de Cuéllar's final criteria, which permitted a range of persons not included in the Spanish census to apply and admitted oral testimony. Morocco kept insisting that it wanted to start immediately Polisario agreed to the criteria. The Moroccans may well have been banking on Polisario's refusal thus giving them a free hand, but to me, in public and to the media they continued to reiterate loudly how anxious they were to implement identification and Polisario should be made to comply with the Security Council decision and participate.

Driss Basri, the all-powerful minister of interior, spoke for Morocco. His working day followed a pattern: golf in the morning accompanied by one of his personal staff and trailing a selection of ministers and top officials with whom he had business to transact. Every shot was dutifully applauded before Basri walked ahead together with one other away from telephones, walls with ears or eavesdropping. It was on the golf course that he and I did serious business. His appointment at the palace came next before his own office. Basri was the king's man of confidence and in a land where loyalty was the paramount virtue he earned rich rewards. His power was only matched by great wealth, ostentatiously displayed, his houses, in Rabat, on the shore, in the countryside, all superabundantly and luxuriously appointed.

Jubilant reception after having negotiated Polisario's
agreement to launch the settlement plan

Basri implemented the king's commands. He himself gave orders, he was not accustomed to accepting any other instructions. The Security Council had mandated that we begin with identifying persons included in the Spanish census. That Basri rejected out of hand at a gathering with full media coverage: it was inconceivable that Sahrawis who campaigned for independence from Spain and were therefore not censused should be excluded – and he pointed to several distinguished Sahrawis in the room. Sahrawis should all have the right to present their case and it was for Polisario to agree the secretary-general's criteria. Polisario still refused, partly because they were convinced that Morocco would deploy overwhelming numbers or whatever other means needed to ensure a referendum in its clear favour. Nor did Polisario see how the new criteria and oral testimony could be convincingly and honestly applied.

By then I had established good relations with the movement's number two. Bachir Mustafa Sayed was the brother of Polisario's charismatic founder and had inherited his brother's mantle when El-Ouali was killed in battle. A man of charm and considerable ability he represented Polisario in dealings with the outside world and in particular the UN. We liked each other and it is, I think, true to say that he trusted me well enough to take a risk. I persuaded Bachir that the identification commission would not be drowned by numbers or bamboozled into accepting false testimony, and Polisario would have their own sheikhs and observers always present. The new criteria posed a problem, it was true but if meticulously applied need not be an insuperable threat. After many, many hours discussion and endless repetition the prospect of agreement flickered but the Polisario, having vigorously denounced Pérez de Cuéllar's last minute proposals, could not now simply say yes. As a solution I proposed that without mentioning the criteria as such they state officially that they agreed to implement the latest Security Council resolution, which referred discreetly to the report containing the criteria. Basri, after first refusing to believe, was hoist in his own petard. To Security Council surprise as much as Morocco's, identification began in 1994.

From Basri's many statements to me it was quite apparent that the Moroccans would never commit to a referendum they might not win decisively; it was equally clear that the Polisario would not willingly submit to a referendum rigged to ensure Morocco's victory. I had no illusion that identification and the remaining settlement plan could be fully implemented with the parties' voluntary cooperation, as mandated. My hope was to use the identification process to tie both sides into the search for an honourable compromise, to build confidence and develop personal relations with a view to arranging constructive talks between the two sides.

Yakub-Khan had made two attempts, both aborted and in effect counter productive. I believed much greater preparation was necessary and that identification could be useful. The procedures developed to identify valid applicants were cumbersome, susceptible to disruption whenever one side or the other saw its prospects endangered but ultimately convincing. The Moroccans presented vast numbers of candidates, the majority of whom looked unlikely to qualify, but Polisario refused to have faith that our identification commission would be able to continue resisting such overwhelming Moroccan pressure. My plan was to keep identification going as long as needed to demonstrate the probable outcome. At the same time I explored the prospect of a negotiated political compromise, the most realistic being regional autonomy.

After two years identification we had processed almost as many people as were in the original Spanish census though only a fraction of the additional candidates presented by Morocco. This was sufficient to guess-estimate the composition of the eventual electoral roll and from that deduce the outcome of a referendum. Basri was not readily convinced that Morocco would not command a decisive majority and Polisario remained nervous when I urged consideration of a compromise settlement. Eventually, after many months unrelenting shuttle diplomacy, I obtained from both sides agreement to talk, with a viable commitment from Polisario to observe total secrecy and Morocco's promise not to include on its team any former Sahrawi supporters, 'traitors' who had changed sides, the two predominant issues that had scuttled every earlier attempt by secretaries-general and representatives to launch negotiation. Equally important I was given absolute assurance by Basri as well as Bachir that they would negotiate in good faith with a view to a political compromise excluding straightforward integration into Morocco off one edge of the table and full independence off the other. Despite numerous hitches as the day approached in the late summer of 1996, the Polisario delegation was received correctly in Rabat and Morocco was represented by Crown Prince Mohamed and Basri. The initial meetings exceeded expectation, and Polisario looked to their audience with the king. But the delegation had to depart Rabat without being received. Basri had become unnerved by the very real progress achieved; he had expected, I am certain in retrospect, that Polisario would not honour some aspect of what had been agreed and he could claim that as reason to break off the negotiation he had claimed to welcome.

In bringing the two sides together on mutually acceptable terms for serious focused discussion I achieved the breakthrough that had eluded the Security Council, the Americans, two secretaries-general and others. I had taken the process as far as my powers permitted, indeed rather further, and it would have been for great power pressure to nudge the parties to commitment. Precisely what Basri dreaded and he deployed all means he could muster to have the negotiations remain unreported to the Security Council, eliminated from the public record and as far as conceivably possible turned into a non-happening. While he had assured me repeatedly of his support for a regional autonomy compromise – indeed that was the only basis on which I could have brought the two sides together – years later, cashiered under Hassan's successor and exiled in Paris, he openly confessed his life-long and visceral opposition to any form of regional autonomy as a threat to the kingdom's integrity.

Basri's could be seen as a serious political misjudgement for which Morocco was to pay a heavy price. The jettisoned talks were followed by clumsy manipulation of the revived identification process ultimately leading to an electoral roll precisely as Polisario desired and with Morocco reduced to invoking an unrealistic appeals procedure. By then I had left the Sahara, hugely disappointed at such a missed opportunity. After long years of continuing regional friction Morocco presented to the Security Council a formal proposal for regional autonomy as its official position, while Polisario clung to a referendum of self-determination with the option of independence. Neither saw reason to compromise.

Farewell to Basri at the secretary-general's
office in New York

185

20 Sarawak revisited, religion and identities

IT HAD ALWAYS BEEN my intention to return to Sarawak for an extended visit when circumstances permitted. Occasional letters assured me that most of my team from Ridan still lived. Kuching when I landed in 1998 was changed but recognisable. A procession near the hotel proclaimed itself as honouring the Anglican church and I trailed behind the bishops bringing up the rear towards the cathedral. In the grounds of the bishop's house, the processors gathered for something to drink and a snack. They were Chinese and Iban and other native Sarawakians. Among a group of Iban I thought I recognised people from the Lemanak and I approached them speaking Iban. A white man speaking Iban perplexed them till one suddenly burst out that it had to be Tuan Ragum (a nickname given me by the Iban) from Ridan. The language came back to me sufficiently to confirm my identity and to ask for their news. They insisted that I visit the Lemanak, where, they said, life was greatly improved and many longhouses had become Christian.

In Simanggang Nanyie assembled nearly all the 'original Ridan' team to welcome me at an emotional and very enjoyable evening. During the days following I went to several of the familiar longhouse villages, now re-sited and splendidly rebuilt, where I was overwhelmed by the generous welcome and hospitality. Penghulu Ancheh of Sebliau was still completing what promised to become an imposing new-style longhouse and I would be their guest of honour at the opening ceremonies, he said, as he embraced me in a very un-Iban display of emotion. I had changed their lives, he added, with tears rolling down his cheek.

From Sebliau I went on a visit to the ulu Undup where I first lived and to which a road had been built. The Wong Padong waterfall, where boats had once to be dragged, was now bridged. Nuli, the schoolmaster who greeted me on first arrival and became my friend, lived nearby in a new house and offered to drive me. We passed Batu Lintang and its tiny bazaar before reaching the impressive Sungai Reboh longhouse where Edwin occupied the headman's bilek. It was a classical longhouse with differences: off the ground but only two or three feet and no livestock underneath to dirty the earth. The house itself was beautifully constructed of fine timber, treated and varnished, and impeccably clean. Edwin greeted me with great warmth and served us tea. We were not given food or anything serious to drink, nor urged to stay the night; this departure from traditional Iban hospitality totally confused me. Then I understood: Edwin did not wish to embarrass Nuli, who had become a Muslim and as such was prohibited from taking food where pork was cooked and being seen to drink alcohol.

As we were leaving Edwin invited me to the place he had acquired in Simanggang when a member of parliament, where he could receive me in traditional style, and he did. That Nuli, of all people, should become Muslim shocked me until I discovered about the political and social changes to which Sarawak was being subjected. The federal government in Kuala Lumpur not only subsidised mosque building and Islamic activities, it deployed a range of inducements to convert to Islam. Nuli had a very intelligent son, by his second marriage, who, if he had a Muslim father, would be awarded the most generous of scholarships and opportunities for higher education. And that was not all. So Nuli adopted Malayness.

Becoming Muslim in the local language was to 'masok Melayu', to become Malay. You acquired a Malay name and dressed in Malay style with a songkok cap always on your head. You were no longer officially classified as Iban or able to lead life as an Iban; unlike becoming Christian, you could not conform to Iban ways, go to a restaurant with your Iban friends, much less drink a glass of beer together. This was not a question of personal faith, it represented a change of identity.

Identity had been a private concern ever since childhood. I grew up uncertain whether I was really Danish, I felt myself English, equally so in Denmark. In America I was considered English, principally because of my speech, but I returned with a strong sense of belonging to Europe. In Sarawak I was part of the British establishment and after being naturalised British awoke to find myself with a Malaysian passport. Being Malaysian seemed unreal, made me feel something of an imposter, and it was as a UNer with a UN laissez-passer that I felt most comfortable 'bien dans mon peau'; after retirement I was happy to acquire a European passport. My personal experience was far from the only identity issue to which I was exposed over the years. In Sarawak I lived with the Iban as they moved from being a tribal people with their distinctive religious beliefs and notions of who they were to becoming progressive Iban in a changing world where many, probably the majority, adopted Christianity. They remained Iban as Christians, had they adopted Islam that would have been impossible since Muslims were considered Malay whatever they might privately believe. In Morocco it was similar: a Moroccan was automatically Muslim, the only recognised exception being the Jewish minority, which had been in the realm for centuries and were known as Moroccan Jews. These were religious identities ascribed to people irrespective of the personal faith element characteristic of Christianity, most especially post-reformation Christianity, and which is taken as determinant in today's international conventions on freedom of religion.

Religion defies neat definition. It has meanings that differ over time and in place. Unlike the western world where protestant Christianity has long been influential and religious faith is treated as a personal matter with the individual free to choose what he or she believes, religion is widely conflated with personal, tribal or national identity. Under human rights conventions of the modern world religion is nowadays officially recognised as a personal matter, an individual right, but that was rarely true in the past and it is far from true everywhere today. Whether it is indubitably best to treat religion as exclusively an individual, personal matter is open to question; religion has often had its principal role in bringing members of a community together, using ritual, art and architecture, language and music, to promote common values and a social bond while marking the most important stages in human life of birth, marriage and death as well as ceremonies to celebrate moments and events affecting the whole community.

Judaism was a classical tribal religion with circumcision as its distinctive tribal scarring. As I learnt from my distraught visitor in the palais, it is still inherited through the mother, but only through the mother, from whom you were born a Jew and expected to conform to Jewish rites. Historically the Jewish people offered sacrifices to their god who, being their god, could be expected to defend their interests. As a tribal religion and identity Judaism had been anything but unique in the region until the Jews convinced themselves that their god, Jahweh, was not merely the only god worthy of worship but actually the only 'true god' and a moral god. In the bid for universal validity Jahweh went beyond the Greeks and Romans whose gods had specific functions such as warfare and fertility, and were for the most part rooted and worshipped in a given locality with appropriate rituals and sacrificial offerings expected of people in that place, even when passing through. Iban religion embodied similar attributes, as a tribal identity and code applying to everyone born to the longhouse community and with sacrificial rites in common, which could even be performed by visitors without reference to what they 'believed'.

The notion of conversion, of personal faith characteristic of Christianity, was novel in distinguishing the individual from the community into which he or she had been born or was living and that it was available to everyone everywhere, as the only true religion, the one truth applicable to all people for all time. As it progressed into the Hellenistic world it absorbed aspects of classical philosophy and thought, alienating itself increasingly from its Semitic origins. It developed a sophisticated theology reconciling monotheistic belief in one god with the divinity of Jesus and the concept of the Trinity, which, centuries later, may have provided a potent incentive for Islam's unqualified recommitment to: 'there is no god but god – and Mohamed is [only] his prophet'.

Islam, closer to the Semitic environment, maintained circumcision and similar food taboos, and, moving away from European influence, proclaimed that Islam not Christianity was the final revelation, the one true religion. The inherited tension between the nominally Christian countries and Islam is exacerbated to this day, because Islam retains what Christendom has lost: a fusion between political identity and religion. Precisely as I experienced it in Malaysia and Morocco and as it manifests itself in the problem western states often have in digesting Muslims, in absorbing them as fully committed citizens so long as Islam emphasises the Ummah, transcending nationality and geography, as the worldwide community to which all Muslims belong and to which they owe loyalty.

My missions to Nigeria, Bahrain and East Pakistan/Bangladesh all related to conflict arising partly from the confusion of political, tribal and religious identity. Biafra, when it sought to secede from Nigeria, was predominantly Ibo and Christian, from which a Biafran identity was being moulded to include some other tribal groups. The Biafrans wanted to be independent of a federation in which the more populous Islamic Hausa-speaking, less well-educated people of the north predominated. It took a Christian from a small middle belt tribe to fight the federal cause 'to keep Nigeria one'. Nigeria remains one but it continues to harbour the fissiparous tensions inevitable in a country imperially assembled from divergent and largely incompatible identities.

The problem in Bahrain was internal to Islam: a straightforward conflict between the Sunni ruling family with Arab ties and a majority of people who were Shia with links to Iran; but it was muddied by Iran's closeness to the United States at the time and Soviet Arab alliances. Neither Nigeria nor Bahrain had consequences similar to East Pakistan when it became

Bangladesh. When the Indian empire achieved independence it was divided between India and Pakistan, as the Muslim homeland. Thousands were killed when they endeavoured to resettle whether in the west where, with the ongoing exception of Kashmir, most frontiers were recognised and in the east where the Bengalis were Muslim. But not all Bengal was Muslim and beyond, on Indian land, lived the Biharis, many of whom were Muslim, who opted to settle in East Pakistan. The Bengalis were fellow Muslims but with a distinct identity and their own language. The Biharis tended to identify with the administrators drawn principally from West Pakistan who were Urdu-speaking. When Bangladesh came into being with West Pakistanis ejected and Bengalis in power, the Biharis found themselves fiercely unwanted. But West Pakistan refused to absorb them as not belonging there and India rejected reabsorbing people who had deliberately selected not to be Indian. A tragic case of religious, tribal and political identity entanglement.

When full retirement from the UN became inevitable I had no wish to stop working, to cease making a contribution and become a waste of space as I had watched in others. A notice in *The Economist* inspired me to put forward my name for an academic post in Boston. The Warburg Chair in International Relations at Simmons College (now University) had been founded to entice a former senior diplomat to spend two years bringing the benefits of diplomatic experience into the ivory tower. Previous incumbents, I discovered, were distinguished US ambassadors, retired, or in one case had been ambassador to Washington, but I applied, and was delighted to be selected in 1998 having the required ambassadorial status as a UN Under-Secretary-General.

Becoming a 'prof' at Simmons College/University, Boston

Academic life in Boston, with a famous named professorship, was as stimulating as it was agreeable. I enjoyed the challenging questions put by uninhibited American students and association with eminent scholars in the Cambridge community and was gratified to be asked to stay beyond the statutory two years. When, sadly, my extended appointment at Simmons came to an end I returned to Europe. I was at dinner with friends in the Haute Savoie; they had also invited a retired German couple and almost inevitably conversation circled round to retirement. I could not help saying, perhaps a little too emphatically, how much I regretted no longer working. That sparked a violent reaction from a fellow guest who told us how relieved she was when she was able to stop as a primary school-teacher – if I had tried that for forty years I would not be saying what I just said.

The ending of formal employment left me free to write. I was commissioned to produce and delivered a monograph about the stalemate in Western Sahara but my heart was in my planned book about the Iban and Sarawak. The return visit had provided the images I needed of what had happened to the scheme at Ridan and how the Iban had evolved in the forty years since I lived among them. Parts of a draft had been in the making for years under the provisional title of *Out of Borneo*, which had to be abandoned immediately after *Out of Africa* was released as a film. Karen Blixen's book had never suggested much beyond the title, it was more to Conrad that I looked and his Lord Jim. My text eventually came together as *Where Hornbills Fly* and its warm reception in Sarawak gave me the greatest satisfaction, greater than London's eulogistic reviews and even the Malaysian government, having already recognized my contributions with a state decoration, honouring me with elevation to 'Dato', approximating to a knighthood, and the distinction of a federal award. With the book I paid tribute to the Iban and especially those who worked beside me in the Lemanak during the early difficult days.

To Africa I paid a different kind of homage. The Nigerian-Biafran civil war had shown me the challenges that young countries face, the involvement in African affairs of powerful governments and the complexities of humanitarian aid. This I chose to capture as a novel, writing under a pseudonym, easily deciphered. Erik Jay's *Under the Sun* is set in (west) Africa and the setting is totally true to life as are most of the characters both African and foreign but I imagined a love interest to make the story more readable and as a diversion from the all-pervading violence. The first publisher to express interest then declined because of the underlying sense of violence that permeated the book, a criticism that would have been inconceivable in the decades following as reports of civil warfare around Africa proliferated.

Being decorated and conferred with the title of Dato

As a change of pace I edited and introduced a work about Britain and the UN; of that my most vivid memory remains the publisher presenting a 'maroon' cover image, having failed to notice that the cover pictured both the Union Jack and the UN flag. *The Struggle for Western Sahara* would inevitably provide my magnum opus. But if the conflict loomed large for me one publisher after another insisted that the minimal level of interest in the Anglophone world was unlikely to justify publication. It proved much more challenging to have the book published – it was almost scuttled at the last moment by the potential threat of libel – than it was to write. Borneo, the African novel and Western Sahara make a biographic trilogy of sorts, which I would label 'Youth' with Conrad in mind, 'Experience' with a sideways glance towards Martin Amis, and 'Diplomacy' with apologies to Harold Nicolson and Henry Kissinger. They sum up the significant stages of my life.

'Do you have any regrets?' a question often asked of the elderly. Of course. It would be absurd not to. That the Saharan autonomy compromise I brokered was not implemented when the moment favoured has to be my biggest regret;

that the dispute drags on at huge cost to thousands of people makes it all the more bitter. At a purely personal level, apart from the many idiocies committed most often because of drink and frustration, my principal regrets are 'sins of omission', what I might have done and failed to do, including failure to apologise when this was warranted and failing to express thanks for all that others did for me in my private life as well as professionally. My professional career afforded me a great deal. The Borneo years were especially challenging; they were equally rewarding, but most marked were the Saharan years. It is often so: only on reaching our highest level of responsibility do we discover, and others observe, both our limitations and what we are capable of. It was a privilege to head a peace-keeping operation, to be conscious of how greatly one's work mattered to many thousands of people. Both the beginnings of professional life, in the jungle, and the ending, in the desert, gave me a powerful sense, not of my own importance but how important for others my work could be. When I failed, I failed those who counted on me. I was fortunate in being able to contribute, largely unscathed, my vision, my time and energy; two colleagues who were my friends, gave their lives in ghastly circumstances while heading missions, one in Iraq, the other in Haiti.

Please do not conclude that my jungle to desert story has any metaphorical implication, fascinating though it was to experience traditional ways of human life at both extremes. At those extremes and on many stops between I enjoyed an extraordinary span of friends. Sadly, an international career, which makes friendship possible in many parts, takes it away in retirement. We are too far apart; convivial evenings reminiscing over two or three glasses are rare. That I miss profoundly. But when I talk to friends from my university days, those who have lived traditional lives, with families, children's godparents, accessibly grouped, I don't begrudge them. I have something richer, more exciting. Not for a moment do I regret having spent most of my useful years serving the UN – not because it was a 'cushy number', which it certainly wasn't always, nor for the 'good life by the lake', which I tasted briefly, but because it was, and is, a cause worth serving enhanced by worldwide exposure and serving alongside others who share that belief. Early idealism never petered out. I came to recognise all too clearly the UN's limitations – it is a relief not always to play the defending champion – but I remain convinced that the Preamble to the Charter is as worthwhile a credo and fine a prayer as any – whatever the bickering sovereign nation statists of this world may say – and worth campaigning for.

It has been a privilege to belong to the post WWII generation that deployed its aspirations for a better future worldwide and achieved so much, but tragic on approaching the end of life to witness so much being dismantled, discarded or deliberately misused, only made worse through the ghastliness spread by Covid 19 and its consequences. It does make the prospect of dying less unattractive and definitely rules out any desire for reincarnation. I have seen too many dead bodies and bits of bodies in various parts of the world to imagine any conscious existence after death whether amid the dubious delights of heaven, Viking, ancient Greek, Iban, Muslim or Christian, or of hell, which would be would be far too overcrowded to cope. My afterlife focuses on the trees I planted some fifty years ago to create a modest park surrounding the three- hundred-year-old chalet in the French Alps, which I bought as an abandoned farmhouse for little money and gradually made pleasingly habitable as time and funds became available. The chalet is now greatly loved by children and grandchildren and it is to them that this book is dedicated. I should like my ashes spread or buried near the pond beneath my magnificent *cedrus atlantica glauca* to fertilise its further soaring Alp and heavenwards.

INDEX

(References to illustrations in bold)